# PERFECT HALVES SERIES

# BOOK 1

# DOUBLE-EDGED

# ROWENA DAWN

SCARLET LEAF
2017

© 2017 by Scarlet Leaf
All rights reserved. No part of this book may be reproduced, stored in a retrieval system or transmitted in any form or by any means without the prior written permission of the publishers, except by a reviewer who may quote brief passages in a review to be printed in a newspaper, magazine or journal.
All characters in this book are fictional, and any resemblance to real persons, living or dead, is coincidental.
Scarlet Leaf has allowed this work to remain exactly as the author intended.

ISBN: 978-1-988397-59-7

PUBLISHED BY SCARLET LEAF

Toronto, Canada

*DISCLAIMER:*
*If while dating on the Internet, someone asks you for money, keep in mind that this is only a story – it is pure fiction and has no relation with reality.*

*DEDICATION:*

*To all the people out there who are
trying to find their soul mates.
Keep safe and keep true!*

# Contents

| | |
|---|---|
| CHAPTER ONE | 11 |
| CHAPTER TWO | 16 |
| CHAPTER THREE | 27 |
| CHAPTER FOUR | 37 |
| CHAPTER FIVE | 41 |
| CHAPTER SIX | 56 |
| CHAPTER SEVEN | 65 |
| CHAPTER EIGHT | 75 |
| CHAPTER NINE | 91 |
| CHAPTER TEN | 99 |
| CHAPTER ELEVEN | 108 |
| CHAPTER TWELVE | 135 |
| CHAPTER THIRTEEN | 165 |
| CHAPTER FOURTEEN | 181 |
| CHAPTER FIFTEEN | 197 |
| CHAPTER SIXTEEN | 207 |
| CHAPTER SEVENTEEN | 214 |
| CHAPTER EIGHTEEN | 220 |
| CHAPTER NINETEEN | 226 |
| CHAPTER TWENTY | 242 |
| EPILOGUE | 246 |

# CHAPTER ONE

*Present day – July 19<sup>th</sup> ...*

The young woman was sitting in a cushy armchair in the lobby, a magazine open on her lap. She pretended being lost in a story she was reading.

Her huge blue slouch-hat was designed to cover half her face and matched the short summer dress, showing off her long, tanned and shapely legs.

A pair of big, black sun-glasses completed the ensemble. She looked like Audrey Hepburn in *Charade*. Hidden behind the black lenses, her eyes carefully watched the people coming to the front desk and speaking to the receptionist.

She had already arranged with the much younger man at the front desk to signal her when the person she was interested in would come. He was supposed to raise his hand, as if he'd said *'just one moment, please'*. Then, he was supposed to turn away for a couple of seconds and check something on the monitor.

Since her watch began, two couples had already passed by the front desk and talked to the clerk. They'd just taken their keys and left immediately, so she didn't bother with them anymore.

Finally, after a few more minutes of impatient waiting, a tall, dark man came to the reception area and addressed the clerk. The clerk nodded and raised his hand, the sign they'd pre-arranged. He checked his computer screen for a couple of seconds, nodded again and then, took a bag from behind the counter and handed it to the man.

He took the bag with a nod and, turned around. His eyes brushed expertly over the people in the lobby. He gave the impression he was just mildly curious, yet she noticed he analyzed everyone carefully. She watched him furtively so she wouldn't expose herself.

She imagined her appearance didn't impress him. After he'd looked her over, from head to toe, taking his time when he swept over her legs, he turned around and went toward the elevators. Probably, he didn't think she posed any kind of danger and he didn't worry about her.

Again, her senses perceived nothing clear about him and that annoyed her much more than before. She realized she had stumbled onto the first person in the world she couldn't read at all. That frustrated and infuriated her to no end.

She'd believed she'd be able to sneak a peek into his mind once she'd be in his presence. It made sense she wouldn't encounter any barriers when she was near. Apparently, she'd been wrong. The man always remained completely opaque to her vision.

When he disappeared from her sight, she stood up with lazy and fluid moves. She laid the magazine on the table next to her armchair, as if she'd had all the time in the world. She smoothened her skirt with long and light strokes, and then, her eyes swept over the hotel lounge, furnished with taste and comfort in mind.

With lazy strides, she walked to the front desk. The clerk beamed at her, warmly. He hurried forward to do her bidding as if the other person at the front desk hadn't mattered at all.

She noticed his rush to serve her and believed the huge tip she'd given him earlier determined his behavior. Yet, something else lay behind the young man's grin. He'd enjoyed their game and even imagined all sorts of thrilling scenarios in his head.

His age, but also her appearance had fueled his imagination. Her hat and big sunglasses, as well as the vague clandestine air of the entire affair she'd involved him in, had made him feel like James Bond or someone similar.

"I'll be leaving this afternoon, I think. I won't be waiting until morning. Of course, I'll pay for tonight, though, no worries," she said to the young receptionist, with an apologetic smile when she realized he'd been hoping that something more would happen and the adventure wouldn't end there.

Yet, she'd been interested in only one scene, and that had already ended, although the result disappointed.

"We're very sorry you're leaving, ma'am. Didn't you like your suite?" the young man inquired, and his worry wiped the smile off his lips.

"Oh, yes, I did, don't worry," she reassured him with a wave of her hand and a bright smile. "But, you see, I've already rented a house on the beach for a few days and I've been thinking I should take advantage of it right now, you know?" she beamed brightly at the clerk again. "There's the sea and a pool just for me... Would you mind preparing the bill before I get back downstairs with my luggage?"

"No, of course, not. Your bill will be ready, ma'am," the man reassured her and rushed to the computer to prepare it.

# CHAPTER TWO

*Always present day – July 19<sup>th</sup> ...*

The young woman left the lobby with her usual lazy stride and headed to the row of shiny elevators, lining the wall on top of a three-step staircase. She pressed the button to call one and waited, playing with her scarf and admiring the geometric motif of the carpet in the hall.

She was deep in her thoughts and failed to notice the dark-haired man behind the column, although the fine hair on her neck stood straight up warning her of danger.

The man watched her unwaveringly, a frown between his eyebrows.

She didn't know he'd heard her conversation with the clerk and in a way, she didn't care. She'd already decided to move on and now, she was anxious to leave everything behind.

She went to her suite and in less than ten minutes, she returned downstairs. She hadn't bothered to unpack upon her arrival that morning and she didn't have much to do to gather her things.

She paid the bill, leaving another sizeable tip for the front desk clerk, who had helped her a lot and asked the valet to bring her rented car to the front of the hotel.

She'd rented a small convertible, nothing fancy, something just to get around. The valet had already lowered the top of the car and that little thoughtful gesture brought a smile on her lips. She felt her vacation had finally started.

The valet put her only suitcase in the trunk and the bag with her laptop in the back seat of the car. He bowed slightly when she gave him a folded banknote, together with a big smile.

Once seated in the car, she turned the key in the ignition first and then she turned on her navigation system, inputting the address of the house she had rented on the shore.

Now, she felt secure enough so she took her hat off and shook her head. Her hair fell all over her shoulders in thick, curly honey-coloured waves and the afternoon sunrays reflected a few shades of red here and there.

Relief set her free. She knew things would get back to normal now and she wouldn't face any more restlessness or unanswered questions. Life as she knew it and loved was back. She had control in her hands and knew beforehand where she stood with the people around her. Happiness for her meant no more uncertainty to drive her crazy and fill her sleepless nights with anxiety.

She drove her car slowly along the hotel driveway and turned onto the road toward the beach. She failed to notice a black SUV, a few cars behind, pulling out and following her. But then, she didn't think to look for something like that.

She drove steadily in her usual prudent manner. She wasn't in a rush. The house would be available to her whenever she got there.

She was on vacation after all. She'd completed the business she had to take care of and, now, there was only the sun, the ocean and her. She would lie on the beach in the morning and swim in the pool in the evening.

She'd already planned to keep far from the world and any kind of stress.

She needed peace and solitude for a change.

She admitted it had been somewhat interesting to taste those uneasy feelings although they stressed her at times. They'd brought some spicy restlessness and she didn't regret she'd felt a little different for a while. It had been somewhat... educational.

Yet, it was nice to be herself again and find her old routine. She welcomed a future when she didn't have to find an explanation for things that weren't meant to be explained.

The vacation house she'd rented wasn't very far from the hotel. It took her only fifteen minutes to arrive at her destination.

She drove in front of the bungalow erected right on the edge of the beach and she stopped her car to admire the little house and the surrounding area for a few moments. She liked it. That was going to be her oasis of peace for the following ten days. The view, as well as the sound and smell of the ocean, made her stop regretting she'd left Montreal and taken a few days off.

After a few minutes, she drove her little convertible under the shelter improvised for parking a car and turned off the engine. She got out of the car and put up the top. She'd paid for insurance but she still didn't want to have problems when she would return the vehicle.

The woman breathed greedily the salty air of the sea. The breeze tousled her hair and she grinned. A brief jolt of pleasure swept over her body. It'd been a while since she took a vacation for more than a couple of days.

She took her suitcase out of the trunk and opened the back door to pick up her laptop. She strolled up the paved road to the house and looked for the keys under the flower pot on the right of the door where the broker had told her to look. She went inside, closing the door behind her.

The interior was everything she'd been promised and more than she'd expected. She never trusted the photos displayed next to rentals and she'd thought the broker was just talking the house up to make her lease it.

Yet, the house was vivid and cozy at the same time. The furniture in the living room appeared light and comfortable.

She left her laptop on the top of the little coffee table and went to have a look at the bedroom.

She needed to climb a flight of stairs to get there but the room pleased her. The sunlight warmed the yellow of the walls and the brick-coloured cover of the bed.

She knew she could find her peace of mind in there. She'd already connected with the house and now, she felt as if she'd always been a part of it.

She left the suitcase on the floor next to the bed. She didn't bother to change out of the designer dress she was wearing. She went out on the patio facing the sea at the back of the house. She wanted to enjoy the rest of the afternoon.

She poured a glass of wine on her way out and picked up her cell phone because she knew he would call. He would always call and she didn't see him breaking his habit just then.

On the patio, she found a few wicker armchairs and an oval table for six. A big colourful umbrella loomed over them. She left her glass on the table and turned to look at the beach.

On the sand, beyond the patio, two deck chairs waited for her on the edge of the pool if she wanted to sunbathe. Just a little farther, maybe a two-minute stroll, she could enjoy the waves of the sea.

She left her cell phone on the table as well and sat in one of the armchairs. She stretched her legs onto another chair and relaxed. The last few days' tension seeped out of her body slowly.

She closed her eyes for a few seconds and let her mind wander. She didn't want to think of anything but disperse the impressions of that day. She wanted them behind in the past where they belonged. She'd already fulfilled her purpose.

She had scarcely had the time to decompress for a couple of minutes that the phone rang. She glanced reluctantly at the display and, as always, it showed *'private number'*. She scowled and her scowl made her look much younger than her years, almost like a spirited teenager.

Experiencing a perverse streak, the woman let the phone ring a few times and only then she answered.

"Hello!"

"Kate, is it you, sweetheart?" the very well known male voice came over the line.

"Yes, it's me, of course," she said trying to cover a growl in her throat.

That was a *stupid* question. *Who else could answer my phone?* It had never happened before.

Besides, in moments like that she simply loathed that word '*sweetheart*'. She was distressed because she couldn't discern sincerity or insincerity in his words. That drove her crazy.

She didn't understand why he was the only person she couldn't read. It was maddening not to know what he was thinking and what his intentions were.

"Thank you, my love, I got it. You are fantastic," he continued and the tone of his voice woke the dormant butterflies in her belly.

His voice was low and hoarse, and made her picture a cowboy holding a glass of whiskey in one hand and a cigar in the other. Probably a reminiscence of her childhood days when she loved to watch westerns. Goosebumps covered her arms whenever she heard his voice, and she resented herself because her IQ dropped to two digits. She'd thought herself smarter than that.

*'Of course, I am,'* she thought, *'fantastically stupid, maybe,'* but she replied something completely different, "Then everything is alright, yes?"

"Yes, my love," he answered and paused for a few seconds. "You sound so close now. I usually can't hear you so well," he said with wonder in his voice.

"Probably, you've got a good line," she replied flippantly and her lips arched in a derisive smile.

Of course, he could hear her better. They were both in the same town, for Christ's sake, but she wasn't about to tell him that. She hadn't gone through all that trouble to reveal such information now.

"Now everything will be all right," he continued in a firm voice. "I'll finish everything here and come to you."

"Don't hurry on my account," she replied without thinking, and then she closed her eyes tight in frustration.

Kate was afraid he would understand what she meant and she wanted a clean break up. She didn't want to drag that so-called relationship any longer.

"What do you mean?" he asked in the same hard voice he used whenever he got angry.

His voice had a lower pitch now and Kate perceived that hint of authority, which she loathed deeply.

Kate didn't like his attitude. He probably thought she would respond to his demanding voice and behave accordingly. That reaction was innate to him and he couldn't censor his words, and yet, she still abhorred it.

"I mean I might have to leave the country for a while, Ryan. Family problems, you know," she said just in passing. "Of course, my phone won't work outside the country as I don't have roaming. I'll call you when I can, all right?" she said in a conciliatory voice.

She didn't feel conciliatory right then but she wanted to end the conversation and cut all ties to him.

Ryan didn't answer anything for a while and silence grew menacing.

"Are you still there?" she asked after almost a minute.

"Yes, I am. I'm here, Kate. And when I say here, that means here," his reply came heatedly.

Not a second later, heavy footsteps sounded on the veranda surrounding the house. Kate glanced there and saw Ryan coming to her. An ugly scowl tugged at the corner of his lips. He turned off his phone. The expression on his face didn't announce anything good.

# CHAPTER THREE

*Three months earlier – April 15th ....*

"Come on, Kate, you must try it. You never have time to go anywhere or to meet someone. That shop of yours is taking up all your time. This is your chance," Ellie tried her best to coerce Kate. She was staring Kate down with her big puppy eyes.

Kate smiled. She couldn't find fault with poor, sweet Ellie. She was always trying to find happiness for everyone else even though her own was questionable. Kate knew Ellie didn't have anyone special in her life.

"I don't know, Ellie," Kate replied with a shrug. Indecision tightened her lips. "You know, there are all sorts of loony people out there," she continued with a large wave of her hand. "And besides, I don't think it's really safe to meet someone on the Internet. I've heard so many stories about everything that could go wrong," Kate explained to Ellie.

Kate didn't truly believe that it was safer outside in the real world than it was to connect with someone on the Internet. There were enough crazy people everywhere, in the streets, shops and bars. She'd read enough minds to know what ugly thoughts crossed people's minds.

"Okay, Kate, maybe you're right," Ellie agreed with her for a moment. "But we both know that you're smart enough to read into things. You have that special touch with people and you'll know if something's wrong. Of course, you won't go meet a guy if he doesn't seem all right," Ellie tried to reassure her. She picked up her tea cup and sipped some of the hot tisane Kate had prepared for her just a few minutes earlier.

"Yes, Ellie, but a guy might seem all right and he might not be, you know that," Kate insisted just to rile Ellie a little. She didn't like anyone mingling in her life. "The bad ones are like that," she said with a wide wave of her hand. "And of course, I'm one of the good girls and that's exactly why I'll choose the worst of them," she joked but Ellie took her at face value.

"Don't be so negative," Ellie replied slapping her arm. "Come on, Katie, let's make a couple of nice salads, as you promised, and then you'll open your computer."

"What's the relation between salads and my computer, Ellie?" Kate simulated misunderstanding just to tease Ellie.

Ellie rolled her eyes and scowled at Kate, "You know what I mean, don't play games with me. We're going to eat and prepare a profile for you at the same time. I know the best dating site."

"Have you tried it?" Kate threw over her shoulder on her way to the kitchen.

"Me? No," Ellie mused and followed her.

"Then how do you know it is the best?" Kate glanced back at her.

"One of my colleagues used it," Ellie explained with large gestures. "And she got married, a little while ago. She said it was the chance of a lifetime," she made sure to add.

"I see, Ellie… Have you thought that she might have been one of the few lucky ones?" Kate asked, reluctantly opening the laptop she'd left on the kitchen counter earlier when she got home. "The statistics are not very encouraging," she continued.

She'd learned that throwing statistics in a conversation always won points. No one bothered to verify her statements and she came up ahead.

Ellie dismissed her reply with a quick wave of her hand and went to gather the ingredients to prepare the salads.

Kate looked after her, not wanting to give in so easy, "You know I'm right, Ellie. Tell me, would you do it, if you were in my place?" she insisted.

"Me? No, of course, not! And you know why? I'm sure you do. It's because I'm not good at reading between the lines. I take everything at face value and that always gets me into trouble. You know it," Ellie explained, reminding to Kate about her bad choices from the past. "But you're not like me, Kate. You're smart and you know people so you do have what it takes for such a thing."

Kate smiled. She couldn't do anything else but smile. Ellie had always put her on a pedestal, and sometimes she felt ashamed because of that. That was one of the reasons she never could refuse Ellie.

"Okay, I imagine I can handle this," she shrugged. "I am pretty sure no one can trace me and find out who I am..." she thought aloud. "Maybe just the town if they know how to use my IP address, I think..." A frown appeared between her eyebrows. "Anyway, I'll not answer back to any wacko out there. I won't give any pertinent information about me..." Kate continued pensively. "Okay, Ellie, now, we'll finally see if I'm smart enough to deal with something like that," Kate concluded and Ellie jumped up and down with glee.

As a matter of fact, Kate had a strange feeling about that whole dating thing. She felt as if something had touched her. It was like a sign that something with deep consequences was about to happen and she didn't like it at all.

Ellie laughed at her concerns and, after they made the salads cheerfully, they went back to the computer.

"Look, this is the site I was telling you about," Ellie showed Kate. "You see, Kate, they have so many questions. You can't get it wrong. You will find just the right guy, I'm telling you," Ellie beamed at Kate.

"Yes, they have questions, but with predefined answers. Look at this here. Do you think any of this is me? What else can I choose?" Kate asked frustrated.

"Yep, you're right," Ellie conceded. "It's a little too rigid."

"And imagine the guys have the same problem. Most of these answers don't apply to me so I suppose any guy filling in this form will find himself in the same situation. Even if he doesn't want to lie, he will. He doesn't have a choice if he wants to continue with the form," Kate said, always frustrated.

"Just choose something close enough. There must be something that might work for you," Ellie insisted. She didn't want Kate give up.

"Yes, I can do that, if I want to create a new me from scratch, there is. But I think that I must choose something. They don't let you move on otherwise," Kate scowled.

They needed about two hours to answer all the questions in the questionnaire. Both were exhausted and only Ellie experienced something like a triumph.

"Now, you have to choose a picture. Choose the best one you have, of course," Ellie thought to specify.

"I don't think so," Kate replied, shaking her head. "I have to choose the worst I have. If someone likes me in that photo, then he's a keeper," she grinned maliciously at Ellie.

"You've always had a very strange sense of humor, Kate," Ellie shook her head astounded. "God, everybody puts the best they have out there. No one will try to attract a possible match with the worst mug shot possible. It's like using your passport photo, Kate, for God's sake," she exploded.

"Maybe," Kate replied indifferent to Ellie's words. "But I like to do things my way, and you know that well, Ellie girl. So, I know exactly which photo should go on my profile. I had one taken last year, immediately after those two weeks when I had the worst flu in the city. In fact, I needed it for my passport, if I remember correctly. I was thinking of going to Mexico on a vacation and then I gave up..." she said pensively. "Yes, I think that's the best photo we should try," she said confidently and started browsing the folders on her computer to find the photo in question. She didn't pay any attention to Ellie who was rolling her eyes in disbelief.

"It's like you don't even want to try," she cried out.

"Au contraire, ma petite! This is me trying," Kate said with determination. "You'll see it's for the best."

Ellie made a few attempts to make Kate change her mind, however nothing swayed Kate from her decision. Ellie should have known better than wasting her breath. Kate was stubborn like a mule when she chose so.

The photo she chose showed a pale Kate. She seemed to have cleaned her face very well – so well that there was no colour left in her cheeks. Only her eyes were standing out, green like the sea, a heritage from her departed mother. Her hair looked unhealthy, flat and dull. At least, she had it dressed in a bun, even though it resembled to a bun her grandmother would have created five or six decades earlier.

Up the photo went onto the profile. Kate didn't budge, of course.

"Now you must wait," Ellie advised her as if she'd had a lot of knowledge about online dating. "You might receive some matches tomorrow but I wouldn't count on that. Why did you choose to be matched with guys from all over the world? I really don't understand. You should have chosen just Montreal, Kate. How would you meet a guy from Australia, for instance?"

"You were talking about the chance of a lifetime, remember? If it's to meet my soul mate," Kate replied playfully, "then, I must consider he might be somewhere at the other end of the world, don't you think? What are the chances to meet him right here, in the city? I'd have met him already," Kate pointed out.

Ellie seemed to have her doubts but she didn't want to contradict Kate. Kate was the clever one between the two of them. She was the one who could feel the pulse in any problem and astonishingly, she could say exactly what a person was capable of, even if everything Ellie knew about that individual pointed in a different direction.

Ellie had never been able to find an explanation to all of that, but she'd learned since the first year of school spent in Kate's company not to ever question her reasoning. Kate always knew better. It was a mystery about the how but Ellie had stopped considering that mystery a long time ago.

# CHAPTER FOUR

*The following day – April 16<sup>th</sup> ...*

Kate turned off the alarm and, with sleepy eyes, checked the notifications on the phone. When she saw several messages in a row, all of them coming from the dating site, she woke up thoroughly. She hadn't expected someone would contact her so soon.

Kate put the phone aside and decided to go through her morning ritual first. She went to the bathroom to take a shower and brush her teeth before checking the messages again.

After she finished with her morning routine, she prepared her breakfast and carried it to the breakfast nook facing the garden.

She ate while scrolling through the messages she'd received. Almost all of them came from the same person, a guy named Ryan, and that surprised her.

She'd got messages from four other guys, and they read only *'hi, how are you?'*

Well, that was a way to start a conversation, she supposed, but she'd expected at least a brief introduction or something…

Kate shrugged and forgot about them. She didn't feel like wasting her time with something so generic. Those guys could have written to anybody after all.

She spooned some cereals and decided to read the messages from Ryan.

Message one: *I've just seen your photo. I simply love your eyes. I'd like to meet you.*

She scowled at the phone. Now she thought better. At least, that '*Hi, how are you?*' was inoffensive enough. This guy, Ryan, took out the artillery from the beginning.

Message two, which had come half an hour after the first one, read: '*When I saw your photo, I literally felt a strong pull in my heart. Please, get in touch with me.*'

She read the message again with wide eyes and said aloud, "Huh! Not so gullible, sorry."

Message three (after another half hour): '*I really think you're the one and I can't wait to meet you. Please, reply!*'

Now, she shook her head in bewilderment and murmured, "This guy is something else." Kate was dumbfounded. She couldn't believe someone could come up with such lame lines.

Message four (another half hour later): *'I do hope you haven't seen any of my messages yet and that's the only reason you haven't answered to me. I know we could have something great going on between us. We are the real deal, sweetheart, believe me.'*

She sipped her coffee and rolled her eyes in disbelief. The guy had taken out the big guns.

Message five (after another thirty minutes – one thing was clear; the guy was precise like clockwork): *'I'm still waiting. I know we two would be good together, sweetie. Just write back.'*

She shrugged dismissively and said aloud again, "Yeah, really?"

Message six (always after thirty minutes – at least he was consistent in timing his messages), *'Still waiting here. I'm here, with my computer open waiting for your reply. Please, answer. From what I read, you are indeed my soul mate.'*

This time she burst into laughter, "Really? Come on, really? This guy is unbelievable."

Shaking her head, Kate returned to her breakfast. She was in no hurry to reply to the messages piling up in her inbox.

She was thrilled a bit, she admitted it. Yet, she also felt uneasy. There was a specific vibe to those messages. Either the guy was desperate or he was a stalker.

Anyway, she had to go to work and didn't have time to analyze those possibilities. Kate was her own boss but she was both a conscious employee and a very strict employer. She didn't like it when her employees were late and she was always careful to be on time herself.

She cleaned her breakfast dishes and left the house to go to her shop. She didn't bother with writing an answer to any of the messages she'd received.

# CHAPTER FIVE

*One month earlier - June 10th ...*

"I'm really sorry, sweetheart," Ryan said in a hoarse voice. "I know I said I'd come and meet you and you know I did buy the plane tickets... I sent you the confirmation email, remember? But you see, now, I do have to go on a business trip in Asia... It's not like I want to do it but...," he let the sentence in suspense.

"Interesting, Ryan. You've never mentioned a business trip before," Kate replied, cutting his explanations short. She wanted to get to the heart of the matter and wasn't willing to let him make a fool out of her.

"Come on, don't be like that," he snapped at her. "You know I have business all around the globe, I've told you so. It's not like I'm sitting on my ass all day doing nothing," he raised his voice annoyed with her curt tone. "I haven't planned any trip, that's true, but, Kate, look, things happen, and I really have to take this trip. You must understand. I'll come and meet you after I come back. You know you can trust me, baby." Ryan tried to cajole her and lowered his husky voice.

"Really? How come?" she replied with sarcasm. "How do I know that?"

"You're saying you don't trust me?" he replied in a mean voice.

"I'm saying I don't even know you, Ryan," Kate said, matching his voice. "Let's face the truth. You don't know me and I don't know you," she pointed out in a businesslike manner.

"A... a... after all these m... m... months...," he stammered, "We've... we've talked on the phone, we... we've even chatted a few times a day... I told you everything there is to know about me.... didn't I? How can you say you don't know me? Are you bullshitting me, Kate? Are you? It's not like I'm sitting on my hands here just waiting for things to happen," he snapped, and his voice showed his anger had escalated. He was practically growling by the end of his tirade.

Ryan's sarcasm was dripping all over her skin and a creepy feeling overwhelmed her. Kate was becoming uncomfortable with the conversation and she decided to end it. After all, it wasn't like her to take abuse of any kind from anyone. She preferred to fight.

"Perfect," she replied keeping a cool and distant tone, "take care of your business trip, Ryan. Sayonara!"

She turned off the phone, having time only to hear a shouted *'What the ...'* but she didn't stop to listen to what he wanted to say. She didn't care about it anymore.

Kate was a bit bewildered, though. She'd been unwisely and unwillingly swept into that strange long-distance relationship, in a matter of a few months. There were times when she believed Ryan had put a spell on her but she knew it wasn't possible.

From the beginning, she'd been uncomfortable with the way they eased into talking about everything and nothing at the same time. It didn't seem natural.

Truth be told, Kate was an outgoing person and usually, she got along with people just fine. She had to be a people person or she couldn't have created and nurtured the shop she had and the clientele she'd acquired.

Yet, in her personal relationships, she'd always kept a certain distance. She wouldn't just open the gate to her inner thoughts and feelings to everyone. Maybe it was because she could read people's minds and was often horrified of what she read in most men's minds.

She'd met a few sweet men, but they'd been too sweet for her taste and too willing to do anything to be liked. Maybe it was true women only said they wanted good guys and yet, in the end, they were attracted to the bad boys.

Kate needed a man who proved to be her equal in everything. She didn't want someone she had to coddle infinitely. She didn't feel like being on her toes all the time and taking care not to hurt their feelings.

No matter how patient she was, Kate didn't see herself as a woman ready to cater to a man's every wish or need. After all, she wanted to be the one pampered, and for that, she needed someone strong and dependable. She was looking for someone able to stand on their own two feet and protect her if necessary, a man who'd provide the care and love she desired.

After she subscribed to the dating site, Kate received messages from five men. After a couple of weeks of conversation through both the website and on the phone, she finally met four of them.

Even while talking to them over the phone, she read their mind. It wasn't difficult. Her mental abilities had honed during the last few years and now she was capable to perceive certain thoughts even at a distance.

The thoughts of two of them had been creepy, although loud and clear. They talked about weird fetishes and obsessions, and that made her want to keep her distance. They were harmless, but they weren't for her. She hardly managed a couple of hours during an evening in their company.

One had been beyond creepy, though. What she read in his mind had disturbed her. She found out he'd already met two other women he'd contacted on two different dating sites and both women had met untimely and horrible deaths at his hands.

Kate had made an anonymous call to the police, and given them a few details about the women's deaths. She'd given them the killer's name and description and left it at that. She was confident police could take it from there.

She didn't want to get involved with the police again. She'd done it once, a few years back, when she was much younger and naïve.

At that time, Kate believed she could use her gift to save the world. She scowled whenever she remembered her idealistic enthusiasm at the time. That experience put a stop to any other thoughts about saving the planet.

Kate couldn't forget how the police officers treated her. They believed she was either a freak or a fraud, and, for a time, they couldn't make up their mind about her. They even insinuated she must have been involved with the killer to know all those ghastly details.

That bitter experience made her reluctant to let anyone know about her gift. Not even people close to her, like Ellie, knew about her special talents.

The other two men from the dating site were harmless. They couldn't hurt a fly. Yet, they weren't for her either. They needed someone stronger to manage their life and accept them as they were. They wanted a woman to mother them and she didn't feel maternal enough to embrace that role.

Kate looked for someone stronger herself. She wanted to meet someone she could rely on and who would make her feel as part of a team. She dreamed of a man who would love her, the woman, and not for playing the role of a grown-up boy's mother.

She needed companionship, but she wouldn't settle just for that. Kate longed for everything supposed to happen in an adult relationship: romance, love, physical connection and trust.

The sixth man who contacted her was Ryan. In the beginning, Ryan insinuated himself in her life with messages sent every thirty minutes for twenty-four hours. When she finally gave in and answered back, he continued with witty chat on the Internet.

The man proved knowledgeable in various areas and was a very pleasant conversationalist. She enjoyed their talks. He showed cultural polish and seemed down to earth. Some times, his attitude revealed his dark side, showing the bad boy beneath the polish. That attracted Kate like a magnet.

In less than a week, they exchanged phone numbers, which she regretted when he began calling her day and night, even though she told him, several times, she would prefer sleeping around two a.m. Time didn't seem important to him. He lived somewhere outside the normal time.

Ryan sent her a few photos and in all of them, he wore big hats or caps. She had only a glimpse of his face or his hair. Asked to describe him, she could only say that he was a dark-haired man, because she'd seen the shadow of a dark beard and a lock of dark hair.

He kept promising to take a new photo and send it to her but, of course, he didn't. Something always interfered and he couldn't do it.

Ryan said he lived in Chicago and gave her a Chicago phone number. Kate called that number twice and got an answering machine every time. She never tried again. She just knew no one would answer and the thought bothered her.

Besides, Ryan kept putting off his coming to Montreal to meet her. He would always say he was in the middle of a big contract and his construction company had promised the client a deadline. He explained his reputation, his most important asset, was on the line and he couldn't afford to lose it.

Kate believed Ryan's story about the contract was a lie too, but not because she could read his mind. Kate couldn't even glimpse into his thoughts.

Ryan was the first man who had succeeded in keeping her away from his private thoughts. Whenever she tried to pry, she had the impression he was frowning and pushing her probing waves away. He couldn't know about her attempts to read his thoughts. Yet, his mind felt something was wrong and kept pushing her away.

When they talked on the phone, she sensed something was not quite right but she couldn't put her finger on why or what.

Kate couldn't explain other things either and they worried her. For instance, she'd expect his calls impatiently. She'd find herself longing to hear his raspy voice and his throaty laughter. He was like a poison that seeped into her blood and she couldn't live without.

Ryan's voice made her feel good, at least most of the time. Sometimes, his voice made her tense, yet she was looking forward to those tense moments as well, and that didn't make a lick of sense.

Kate was torn in two directions. On one hand, she needed to stay in contact with him. It was vital to her well-being, although she couldn't say why. On the other hand, she didn't want to hear another word from Ryan and wanted him to stop calling her. His charming ways and sweet words, which would turn into sarcasm in the blink of an eye, overwhelmed her. He would soak her with his arctic condescendence and she felt like decking him.

Kate grew restless during the last few weeks and now she questioned her own wishes. She felt trapped in a maze and couldn't find her way out.

***

Ryan kept calling and leaving voicemails throughout the day. He implored her to pick up the phone and talk to him. He apologized in writing. He sent several emails to excuse his outburst.

He explained that he was just very tired and stressed out because he'd had too many projects in development but he didn't intend to snap at her. It had been just a knee-jerk reaction. His fervent wish was to meet her and because he couldn't do it right then was driving him crazy.

Kate ignored everything until later in the evening. She was tired herself and didn't feel like dealing with him and his moods. Only after nine in the evening, she finally answered to one of his repetitive calls.

"Oh, my love, I didn't mean to upset you," Ryan spoke fast. He seemed afraid she'd change her mind and hang up. "I know it's not your fault everything went awry, but, please, understand I'm just very tired and upset because I can't do what I actually want to do... That's all."

"Meaning?" Kate asked in a calm voice.

She'd decided to keep cool like a cucumber so he couldn't manipulate her emotions anymore. For a few moments, only his shallow breathing filled the line.

She was almost sure he would end the discussion there but he proved her wrong.

"I mean I just want to see you so much and I can't wait to be with you. Do you realize how good we'd be together? I can't wait to have a chance to let my fingers wander all over your skin…"

"Don't tell me you're thinking of phone sex right now??!!" she cut him off in awe.

That was something new. He'd tried a lot of things but not sex talk.

"What do you mean by '*now*'?" Ryan asked with impatience. "I've been dreaming of you for so many days… Of course, I'd love to enjoy you…"

"I'm not a cake…" she interrupted him in a cold voice only to be interrupted at her turn.

"Come on, Kate. Don't tell me you're not thinking of making love to me? I wouldn't have thought you'd be a prude," he snapped at her.

She grinned. He'd forgotten about speaking in a sweet voice and his sarcasm showed once more.

"Of course, I'm not a prude. But I don't know," she said in a flat voice to show him the subject was unimportant.

"Kate!" he bit out and she could hear him gnash his teeth.

"Ryan!" she replied, imitating his tone.

Ryan burst into laughter and said, "You're so good for me, Kate. Baby, you truly are the one. And you do know it." he finished with triumph in his voice.

His laughter felt like fingers touching her spine softly, tracing every ending of her nerves, and she unwillingly shivered. He didn't say anything in explicit words, yet he was touching her erotically right then and her body wondered how the real deal would feel.

Something felt wrong, though. A weird sensation churned her stomach and that always warned her something bad would happen or things weren't what they seemed.

Ryan didn't verbally abuse her, even though sometimes his voice made her feel that way. He would push until he got what he wanted.

Most of the time, their strange relationship seemed great, even though it was long-distance but, now and then, Kate felt like a pawn in a chess game and she resented it deeply. She prided herself with the control she had over her life and actions, and she loathed Ryan's manipulation.

"Still there, baby?" Ryan's voice reached her. His words pulled her back from her woolgathering.

"Yes, still here, but I do have something to do right now and unfortunately I can't stay on the phone any longer. Have a nice trip, Ryan, talk to you later," her words tumbled one after the other. She wanted to break the connection between the two of them.

"Is this your way of punishing me?" Ryan inquired, displeasure ringing in his voice.

"No, no, it isn't. It's just that I do have to go. We'll talk later, anyway, won't we?" she tried to appease him, and then, she felt like slapping herself silly.

"Yeah, we will," Ryan said implacably and his words made her shiver.

Kate turned off the phone and shrugged nonchalantly. She was a fatalist at heart. She knew she could only alter her journey, not her destiny. What she wouldn't do was to alter who she was.

# CHAPTER SIX

*Three days earlier, a few hours after midnight – July 16$^{th}$ ...*

"You know I wouldn't ask you to give me money if I'd had another solution," Ryan practically growled over the phone. "I've never asked you for anything before and I'll give it back to you. I'm a man of my word, Kate," he said through his tight teeth.

"You can growl, Ryan, if it makes you feel better, I really don't care. I don't mix love, as you call it, with money," Kate replied with detachment.

She was determined not to yield to any shady requests. She'd already done her research on the Internet and knew about the scams going around. Ryan's modus operandi fell in that vein.

Now everything made sense: the phone calls at all hours of the day and night just to wear her out; his excuses for not being able to come and meet her face to face.... And now the request for nine thousand dollars...

He called her at five a.m., probably to get her while she was asleep and unable to make safe decisions. *As if I'd be so weak*, she scoffed.

Discovering the truth was heartbreaking, but then she'd never expected something would come out of their weird relationship. Lessons were learnt all the time and some of them were painful. She could live with that.

"It's not like that," Ryan squeezed through his teeth. He did make serious efforts not to explode. "I just have a problem right now. I've told you they froze my account in the States. I'll get back and solve this issue in a couple of weeks. You'll have your money back, with interest, I promise," he tried again.

"I'm not a bank, Ryan. I can't lend you so much money," she said in the same businesslike voice.

"I've asked for a measly couple of thousand not tens of thousands, Kate. I'm sure you can afford it. Of course, if you want to help me out. It's not like you're a pauper, for God's sake! I know you're not." He took a deep breath and continued in a calmer voice, "Kate, I do think we have a truly good relationship.

We're going to be together forever, and build something lasting. Am I wrong?" Ryan inquired in a tired voice.

"Now, it's my turn to ask you why you condition the existence of our relationship to my giving you the money," she asked calmly.

"I'm not doing that, Kate, and you know it," he bit down. "You know what? I don't get it. How can you be such a cold fish when I tell you I have a serious problem and only you can help me? I wouldn't have called so early, but I didn't have a choice. Your money is what I need to solve this issue now and leave from this God forsaken country. I'll finally come to you, baby. We'll be together, as we've always wanted, Kate," he tried a different approach to convince her.

"Maybe it's because I don't believe you when you say there's a problem, Ryan. It seems too convenient," Kate replied in the same cold voice.

"So, you finally admit you don't trust me," he practically bellowed.

"If the shoe fits...," she said softly.

"So, all this time... all this time I've shown you what's in my heart, what I'm feeling and thinking and …. And you've just fooled me ...," Ryan started to say but was interrupted.

"Not really. I've just been myself. I haven't lied to you, not even once. I haven't gone on saying you were my soul mate and we'd be together forever and ever..."

"So, you're saying I've lied to you," he hissed through his clenched teeth.

*He'll definitely ground his teeth to powder*, Kate thought.

"Well, it seems so, yes," Kate admitted without remorse.

"Why? Just because I asked for your help now?" Ryan asked caustically. "I'm good enough to be led around but not good enough to help, huh!" he said bitterly.

"Ryan, you didn't just demand my help, if you remember. You ordered. You didn't ask for it. And anyway, usually people at least meet first, for a couple of times. They talk face to face before going into things like asking for money. No one is doing something like that with good intentions, to be honest," Kate bit out.

"I've had no choice! No choice! That's all! Do you understand me? No choice! If I'd had one, I wouldn't have asked you for the fucking money now, would I?" Ryan replied crossly, spitting every word.

"I don't have a reason to believe there's even a problem," Kate repeated before Ryan rudely interrupted her.

"You're the first woman in my life who's played havoc with my blood pressure, Kate, and that since the beginning. There's always something with you. I've never allowed any woman to do that to me. It's something with you, you know?" Ryan said meanly.

"Since the beginning, you say?" Kate replied softly.

"Yes, since the beginning. You've heard correctly. You've always had to analyze everything I was saying, to doubt everything...."

"I think I've had good reasons." Kate interrupted him again. "You just come out of nowhere, declaring your undying love for me. Come on! You haven't even met me. You just read one stupid questionnaire on that site and you fell in love head over heels. Maybe that works with other women, but I'm not so naïve, Ryan. I don't buy into this. You should have been more original than that," Kate replied cattily.

"Then why have you continued to talk to me if you believed I was a fraud? What was the point?" Ryan asked in a tired and somehow defeated voice.

She didn't expect it from him. He wasn't the man to admit defeat. His stubbornness wouldn't allow him to surrender.

"Curiosity, maybe?" she confessed.

"Curiosity!!!" Ryan shouted in disbelief. "I bared my heart and mind to you and now you come and say you were just curious?"

"Yelling at me won't help with your *'problem'*, Ryan," Kate replied sarcastically. "It will simply make me finish this stupid conversation, which shouldn't have taken place to begin with." Kate's tone was flat to make him understand she didn't care what he chose.

"Stupid conversation, huh?" Ryan murmured. "So, I call and tell you I need your help to defend my freedom and you take it like a stupid conversation. Now, the question is who's been playing who for the last few months, Kate? It hasn't been me, for sure," he concluded.

"Not me, Ryan," she argued. "I've always been myself. I've never professed my undying love. I've never said those worn out '*I love you*' words, people throw left and right," Kate replied flatly.

"But you know I've loved you all this time…," Ryan tried to say but she didn't give him time to finish.

"I know?" Kate inquired. "How could I know, Ryan?"

"Because I've told you so!" Ryan bellowed with exasperation.

She moved the phone away from her ear and stared at it. The man sounded like a howling wolf. He'd probably lost what little patience he'd ever had. In fairness, he didn't seem to have much of that in stock.

She waited a few seconds, and then she returned the phone to her ear and said, "You told me so. Yes, anybody can say that. It's not difficult to say those three tiny words."

"You're such a piece of work, Kate. I can't believe I fell for such a cold-hearted bitch…," Ryan squeezed in before Kate angrily interrupted him.

"Now, you've done it. See you around," she snapped and disconnected the call.

She shook her head in disbelief. The man had the gumption to ask a lot of money, because no matter what he said nine thousand, even Canadian dollars, meant a lot. On top of that, he dared to shout at her at the same time.

She felt she'd fallen in a parallel universe. In the real world, such things never happened or at least not to her.

Kate decided to forget about him and threw the cell phone back in her bag with a nervous gesture. She left her bag in the living-room, far from her bedroom.

On her way back to bed, she heard the phone ringing again but she didn't care to verify whether it was Ryan or not. *As if there's a doubt*, she shrugged. No one else would call her at that hour.

Kate had a lot of things planned for the next morning and she didn't want to waste what was left of her night on that so-called relationship. She needed to write it off and move on with her life.

Yet, back in her cozy bed, Kate's thoughts swarmed around that surreal conversation. She hadn't been able to read Ryan's mind, which was a given already. Yet, his panic was palpable. Ryan had appeared ridden with anxiety, anger and disbelief when she refused to give him the money.

Kate couldn't believe Ryan considered their relationship real, yet she sensed it in him and that made no sense to her. Kate's conclusion leaned toward him being a scammer. Still, a scammer wouldn't show panic or pain and she'd felt both. Her mind reading abilities didn't work with him but her empathy did. Now, she was thoroughly confused with the wide range of emotions coming from Ryan.

Wary, Kate tried to put the conversation with Ryan aside. She made efforts to quiet her mind and fall asleep but, after an hour, she gave up.

The feeling something bad would happen to Ryan and she'd be the instrument of his misfortune bothered her. She hated herself for allowing his words influence her.

Kate got out of bed and went to the kitchen where she turned on the coffee maker. While waiting for the coffee to brew, she watched out of the window.

Her garden basked in the light of the moon, and beaconed her outside. Before leaving the kitchen, she saw the book she was reading lying on the corner of her kitchen table and picked it up.

The night air was warm indeed, and the flower scents soothed her. Her house wasn't very far from the heavy traffic streets, yet only the buzz of insects reached Kate's ears. Somewhere in a distance, an owl hooted and made her smile.

Kate opened her book to read. The book had interested her very much, but now, she couldn't focus on the words. She gave up and sipped her coffee, letting her mind wander to everything and nothing in particular.

## CHAPTER SEVEN

*Always three days earlier minus a few hours – July 16*

After spending a couple of hours in the garden, Kate returned inside for a shower. She had to get ready for work and needed to hurry if she didn't want to be late.

Kate was resigned to being a little sluggish that day. She hadn't slept enough, and her mind had kept chasing ideas, without reaching a conclusion, and that upset her. As she needed to compensate for her lack of sleep, she drank more coffee.

Kate turned the shower on and the warm water stroked her skin. It felt heavenly and she forgot about getting on with her day. Only when the water turned to ice, did she turn the shower off.

Curiosity was one of her faults, so, before leaving the house, she checked her phone. As expected, the display showed several voicemails and at least seventeen missed calls. Ryan had turned into a busy bee during the hours she procrastinated. He'd been calling and texting her like crazy.

Kate shrugged. She left without returning any of his calls or listening to any of the voicemails. Later, during the day, she would have enough time to see what he wanted or what else he was saying to get what he wanted.

***

The morning dragged on and the hours seemed longer. Time slowed down and moved at a snail's pace.

Kate longed for her bed. She visualised herself getting between cool sheets and closing her eyes in sheer bliss. After playing that game a few times, she decided to leave the shop and go home if she did't get better by two p.m.

She sent a few '*sweet*' thoughts in Ryan's direction. She had to thank him for ruining her night's sleep and, subsequently, her day at work.

After muttering a few choice words with a specific address, she continued checking the inventory. She needed to restock soon or she would disappoint a few of her loyal customers.

"Kate, do you know your phone has been ringing for hours?" Alice's exasperated voice came from behind her and Kate winced.

She turned to Alice and looked at her confused. She didn't understand what Alice was saying.

Alice was her most reliable employee and a good friend, as well. She'd been working for Kate from the beginning, when the little shop, which she named *'Just Magic'*, opened its doors before a very curious and cautious clientele.

Alice was not only reliable, but had very good people skills. She knew how to create the atmosphere of magic their customers expected when they crossed the threshold into her shop.

Alice had the gift to frame every sentence in such a way that people truly bought into the magical aura of the shop. Yet, she never said anything directly related to magic or witchcraft.

People needed to believe in magic and that axiom put the idea of such a shop in Kate's mind. Kate knew most of the people coming into her *'magic'* shop came to buy into the illusion of an enchanted world. She made a good profit from that, although it wasn't her only goal. She knew their strong belief in those illusions helped them put up with severe and demanding aspects of their life.

The young shop owner didn't deceive anyone. She just sold her products. What the clients chose to think about those products and what powers they attached to them was their business and not hers.

She sold potpourris, amulets, hand-made soaps and shampoos, hand-creams and flower arrangements. She couldn't be blamed because people thought that the items found in her store had mystical powers and would bring love or prosperity into their lives.

Some of the customers looked at her sideways, sizing her up, as if they'd expected her to sprout wings. Some people believed she was a witch because of the herbal and floral arrangements, but also because of the collection of artifacts she displayed in a case near the cashier.

She also displayed some glass fairies and dragons, created by a young artist who lived near Montreal. People were in awe before them and a lot of customers came from afar just to buy them.

Kate contemplated busily the slices of life crossing her little shop when she realized Alice was still looking at her, waiting for an answer. She couldn't remember what Alice had asked.

"Oh, I'm sorry, Alice, just woolgathering. My brain is in a fog this morning," Kate apologized and rubbed her eyes.

"Not a problem, Kate," Alice waved her concern away. "Is there something I could do for you? It's not like you to be so out of sorts," Alice replied with concern.

Alice knew her boss well. Kate was the epitome of energy and good cheer and she'd never looked so exhausted.

"No, no problems, don't worry," Kate patted Alice's arm. "I just had a bad night and didn't get enough sleep, Alice, that's all. Now, I'm dragging my feet and I'm not capable of anything," she shook her head morosely. "I think I should just call it a day and go home. I don't think I'll be able to get anything done today. Would you be all right if I left?" Kate inquired with apprehension.

She knew afternoons and evenings usually brought more people into the store and sometimes it was crowded in there. Normally, two people were necessary to attend the customers.

"Don't worry, Kate. I've got everything under control and remember, Jeanne is supposed to come at four. We're covered," Alice reassured her and patted her arm.

"Yes, I forgot about that," Kate admitted with worry in her voice.

She never thought she'd ever forget her employees' schedule. She was a businesswoman after all.

She shook her head again to clear it up and said to Alice, "I'll have to come back in the evening, though, to close the shop. You finish at six."

"I can stay till nine, if it's all right with you, and close the shop myself," Alice offered kindly.

Staying over was no trouble at all. Alice knew Kate paid fairly and she needed the money. Life seemed to become more and more expensive every day.

"Would you? Would you stay until closing time? I trust you can close the shop and make the deposit at the bank," Kate jumped at the opportunity.

"Of course, I can, Kate. I haven't made any plans for tonight, no problem. I can close the shop. I'll also make the bank deposit, no worries," she waved her hand with reassurance.

"Great! Then, I'll just go home to bed. I need to sleep a couple of hours at least, I think, and get back to my normal self.

Tomorrow, I'll be fine, you'll see. That's all I need, a little sleep, and I'll be perfect," Kate rumbled.

"Don't worry about anything and just go home and rest," Alice slid her arm over Kate's shoulders and directed her toward the office in the back. "I'll close and make the bank deposit and I'll see you tomorrow when I come at ten, all right?"

"Thank you, Alice, you're a lifesaver," Kate replied enthusiastically.

"Dramatic much?" Alice said bursting into laughter, and patted Kate's shoulder playfully.

"You don't even know, Alice. I do appreciate your help today, you know that," she said and headed toward her office to gather her things.

"By the way, I think you should take a vacation, Kate," Alice shouted after her in a serious voice.

Kate turned and looked at her. Alice looked serious.

"You're exhausted, Kate. I've been working for you for four years now, I think, and I've never known you to go anywhere for more than a weekend. You can't go on like this, you know. You do need a longer break to rest and relax, Kate. Your body needs some decompression, to recharge batteries. I don't think one weekend here and there counts. You can't burn the candle at both ends. I'd book a vacation if I were you, Kate. It's no big deal for me to take care of things here while you're away. We can work out the schedule for the shop just fine," Alice explained and watched her expectantly.

Alice didn't think only about her financial situation. She was also concerned about her boss and friend. Kate had worked hard for years and although she was young and healthy, human body had limits.

"I'll think about it..." Kate replied. "I know, you're right," Kate said quickly and put up her hand when she noticed that Alice wanted to interject. "I promise to think about it and take a vacation soon, you'll see."

"All right, boss. It's your call," Alice said and turned to leave.

"Oh, God, you know I hate to hear that boss thing," Kate retorted with dismay.

"Just joking, Kate," Alice glanced back at her and laughed joyfully. Her laughter brought a smile on Kate's lips as well.

# CHAPTER EIGHT

*A little over two days earlier... July 17th*

Kate arrived at home after a grueling drive. She parked her car and went inside the house. She took her shoes off as soon as she closed the front door behind her. She needed to feel free and was tired to bones.

She threw her bag onto the coffee table and turned around to go into the kitchen. After a few steps, she hesitated. She went back and took her cell phone out of her bag and checked the missed calls. There were about fifteen more.

Ryan had made call after call and left a voicemail every single time. Kate wondered why he wouldn't give up. She would have.

Kate threw the phone back on the table and went to the kitchen where she poured herself a tall glass of orange juice. She drank it slowly, right there, leaning on the counter. After she enjoyed the last drop, she decided to go through voicemails and delete them.

Kate listened to the first two voicemails. An angry Ryan shouted to pick up the damn phone and listen to him. She shrugged and deleted the messages. His tone was far too abusive for a guy who wanted a favor from her.

She didn't bother to listen to the following four. She imagined that they would be on the same line, as Ryan left them very close to the first two. Ryan hadn't had the time to calm down.

She listened to the beginning of the fifth. Now, a sweet Ryan tried to cajole her to call him back. He said he hoped things hadn't changed between them and they still had something to share together. His tone was warm and charming, probably because he realized she wouldn't answer positively to his bellowing. The guy was trying to worm his way back into her heart.

Of course, after a few more sweet and cajoling voicemails, he lost his patience again, '*Answer the damn phone, Kate!*'

Kate shrugged again and then, she told herself she'd been doing that often lately. It was already ingrained in her being. She shrugged once more and then, decisively, she erased all the voicemails and text messages he'd sent. She had enough and didn't want to hear his voice anymore.

She turned the phone off and left it on the table in the dining-room. With long strides, she went to the bedroom, where she yanked her clothes off and got between the cool sheets, exactly as she'd imagined earlier. Soon enough, she fell into a fitful sleep and slept for about three hours.

Kate had a lot of dreams and their protagonist was Ryan. She saw him in all sorts of bad situations, each one worse than the one before. A few times, she dreamed he lay on a dirty floor, blood all over him, and his chest unmoving. One dream flew into another and then another. It was like a ball rolling down the hill and she couldn't stop any of it.

After a fretful sleep, Kate woke up foggy, restless and more out of sorts than before. She rubbed her eyes and hesitantly got out of bed and went to have a shower. She felt clammy all over and she wrinkled her nose when she smelled the sweat coating her skin.

\*\*\*

Kate prepared a light repast, taking her time with insignificant details. She crowded a plate with the two halves of a grilled cheese sandwich and the quarters of an orange she'd peeled carefully.

Afterwards, she went out onto the deck. First, she'd reluctantly made a detour to pick up the phone left on the table in the dining room.

Kate ate her sandwich, yet she kept looking at her phone sideways, as if it had grown horns. She didn't want to touch it. On one hand, she wanted to will the phone to ring but, on the other, she dreaded it.

She'd never been so uncertain of something in her entire life and that annoyed her. She loathed herself for being so hesitant.

Kate understood the troublesome dreams played a major role in how she was feeling. Her analytical mind told her she should take a step back to prudently reconsider everything from a fresh perspective. Even so, she couldn't get over the bothering thought that her decision would have a major effect upon

Ryan's life, and in ways she couldn't even fathom.

Kate allowed herself to fall prey to Ryan's game and she hated herself for that. She was almost sure he tried to scam her. She was a rational woman and even if she worried after having all those dreams, she couldn't just discard her common sense.

The beep of the phone startled her. She checked and sure enough, another text message from Ryan had come.

She hadn't checked the others yet but she decided to skip them and go directly to that one. It read, *'Please, sweetheart, understand, I wouldn't ask this from you if I'd had another choice. I need you to help me now. I need your help. There's no one else I can turn to. I promise you can trust me!'*

After she read the message, Kate snorted inelegantly, something she'd tried to outgrow for a long time. As a child, her mother would always remind her that girls shouldn't behave that way. That was another habit too engrained in her personality to change it now. She put the phone back on the tray, and she returned to her cumbersome thoughts.

Kate knew she still needed to decide and she didn't want to let Ryan sway her just because of the anxiety over her dreams, which made her feel somewhat guilty.

Normally, she wouldn't discount her dreams. She knew her dreams had a way of telling her something important. However, she believed she needed a clear head not just intuition to make her decision.

Kate knew where she stood financially. As a businesswoman, she was very careful with her finances. She reckoned the amount Ryan asked wouldn't beggar her if he turned out to be a scammer. She'd make the money back in a matter of days.

Financial means notwithstanding, two facts concerned and disconcerted her. First, everything sounded too much like the scams she'd read about on the Internet. More than anything, Kate hated to be taken for a sucker. She reviled it when people looked at her and took her for an easy mark because of her youth. Besides, the amount Ryan requested was just under the ten thousand mark, just good to go unnoticed by authorities. She'd have felt more assured, if he had asked ten or eleven thousand.

The second thing, in complete contradiction with the first one, was her deep concern for Ryan. She was almost convinced he was in trouble. Even discounting her dreams, he did seem desperate and on the edge.

She assumed a scammer would have already given up. He'd mark her name under the losses header and move on, looking for an easier mark. That made her believe Ryan didn't run a scam, but he was in an extremely bad situation, and she should try to help him, particularly because she had the means to do it.

Now, if she thought better, in the great scheme of things, she'd never risked anything. She'd never risked either money or her heart.

Kate didn't consider the opening of the shop a real risk. When she opened it, she knew she'd still have her livelihood, even if everything went awry and her business went under. The shop was just a dream come true. Something she loved. Besides, she planned it carefully and made lots of market studies before launching it.

Her parents left her very well off when they died in a car accident almost ten years ago. Kate had wisely invested the money in various funds along the years. She hadn't been greedy and had chosen the safest funds. They might not have brought her a big return per year, but they were secure. Her caution hadn't been in vain. The dive the market had taken a few years before didn't even make a noticeable dent in her funds. She imagined she could play a little risky for once.

Suddenly, Kate realized she did want to give Ryan the money. That shocked her, although she suspected she'd nurtured that idea in her subconscious all the time.

Kate knew her decision was absolutely crazy. She considered it as a smart investment, though. She would find out Ryan's true story and she would feel better knowing she'd done her best to help him if he needed help.

Kate liked being honest with herself. She admitted she'd come to have feelings for him, although she wasn't sure he deserved either her help or her feelings. The admission stunned Kate. She'd never thought she'd develop feelings for a man she'd never seen.

She felt attracted to him or, more accurately, to his voice and his laughter. She liked talking and arguing with him all the time. Almost everything was an argument with Ryan, and a very vocal one.

Both enjoyed those loud conversations. It felt good when they arrived at the same conclusion after a passionate battle of wits.

Kate liked it when Ryan lost his patience and he did, every single time. His patience was in a very short supply although he made efforts to keep his cool as much as possible. Whenever he lost his calm, he'd start speaking through gritted teeth or growling like a wolf.

That amused Kate. His growling sounded primitive, and, somehow, aroused her. It sounded close to a mating ritual and even though she'd been reluctant to admit it to him, she did think of him in that light a time or two. His voice wreaked havoc on her system and made her skin tingle. She didn't like her response to such stimulus. She'd always prided herself with her cold and detached reasoning.

Anyway, Kate resolved to give him the money, and she felt at peace. She made the decision with open eyes. She was prepared not to see any of the money back. She just wanted to make sure she'd done the right thing and could live with herself without regrets and unanswered questions.

Once the decision made, she picked up the phone and replied to Ryan's last message. She didn't bother to read his previous message but wrote, *'Okay, I'll give you the money. How do you propose we do this?'*

In a few seconds, the phone rang and the display showed private number. Only Ryan called her with private number. *The man must have been waiting with the phone in his hand,* she mused.

"Hello, Ryan. I see you've got my message," she greeted him in clipped words. She wanted him to understand everything was just business from that moment on.

"Baby, I've just known you wouldn't let me down. I knew you couldn't give up on me any more than I could give up on you," Ryan almost shouted, his words tumbling one onto another. His joy was evident in every syllable.

"It's not necessary to try so hard, Ryan. I've already said I'd give you the money," Kate replied dismissively.

"What are you saying, Kate? You're saying I'm lying or what?" Ryan shouted back, his tone rising toward the end of the last sentence.

"I'm just saying you've got yourself a deal and it's not necessary to try to charm me anymore," Kate replied unaffected by his outburst.

"So, we're still at the scamming phase, I see," Ryan said bitterly.

Kate discerned a certain resignation in his voice but she resolved she'd already given in by offering him the money, so she wouldn't give in more than that.

She steeled her heart against the pain evident in his words and went back to the problem in question. "How do you want to do it?" she repeated, as if everything had been only business for her.

"All right, you win for the moment," Ryan said with tired resignation. "You win because I need your help and it's not worth having a fight right now. But you won't always win, Kate. You'll see I haven't tried to scam you and you'll be sorry for thinking so low of me," he replied with sadness.

"All right, then. Till then, though, how do you want to do it?" she stubbornly said once more. She didn't want to let him get to her again.

"You could send it by Western Union. I'll give you the name of a guy I know here…"

"No. I won't send the money to a guy I've never heard of, Ryan, and most definitely I won't send such a big amount through Western Union," she cut him off decisively.

"But I can't use a bank account for a transfer. That's not an option, Kate. There's no other way but Western Union," he explained.

"Yes, there is. Tell me the name of the hotel where you're staying and I'll have someone deliver the money at the front desk in forty-eight or seventy-two hours, maximum." Kate replied, always businesslike.

Ryan didn't reply for a few moments. She could hear his breathing and the static on the line but that was all. Kate waited patiently, though. The ball was in his court now and she waited for him to make up his mind. Anyway, she would stick with her solution.

"Are you sure that's how you want to do it?" Ryan asked hesitantly.

*That's something new*, she mused. She'd never heard him hesitate, in any circumstance.

"Yes," she replied.

"All right, then," he said wearily. "We'll do it your way."

'*Like you had a choice,*' she thought derisively but kept her mouth shut.

After a few moments of silence, she asked him again, "So, to what hotel should I send the messenger?"

"The Majestic," he said, his voice as businesslike as hers now.

Ryan seemed to have finally understood she wanted to keep things like that, just a deal between two parties, no feelings involved in the transaction, nothing.

"All right, then. I'll let you know when to go and get your money. It might take a little over forty-eight hours but no more than seventy-two, if I arrange everything in due time," she specified, making sure she had a reserve of time on her side.

"I've survived until now, I'll survive three more days, I think," he said. "You can't imagine how much I appreciate...," he started to express his gratitude but she didn't give him the chance.

"Yeah, I know," she interrupted him. "I'll go now because I have to arrange a few things. I'll send you a message on the phone when you're supposed to go and get your money."

"Thank you, baby, you can't imagine..."

"All right, I understand already," she interrupted him again, in an angry voice. "I have to go, bye."

"But...," Ryan started but stopped when he realized she'd already disconnected the call and he spoke to the static.

He looked at his phone gnashing his teeth and then threw it furiously on the bed nearby.

"Will she do it?" Adam asked him tentatively, afraid to raise his ire.

Ryan turned to him, his hands braced on his hips. He bowed his head and closed his eyes, his stance speaking of defeat. He didn't say anything for a few moments. Then, he looked at Adam and answered, "Yeah, she'll do it."

He turned around thinking of going out when Adam spoke again, "You think you blew it, don't you?"

Ryan stopped with his hand on the knob and then nodded. He replied quietly, "Well, it seems that way. By now, she's sure I'm a scammer."

"But then why would she give you the money?" Adam wondered.

"The hell if I know, Adam… The hell, if I know…. Would you be all right if I go out for about an hour?" Ryan asked, his hand always on the knob. He couldn't wait to get out of the room.

"No worries, pal. I'll be fine, no problem. Go out, you've been cooped in here for the last two days and I think you're about to go nuts," Adam replied and laughed, although his laughter seemed forced.

"I'm getting there," Ryan said and left the small room.

The room had smothered him for the last few hours and he needed a breath of fresh air. He also needed to think about Kate and her sudden change of heart, which he didn't understand. He'd hoped to persuade her, that was true, but he'd been sure he'd need much more time to do it.

# CHAPTER NINE

*Two days earlier - July 17th*

Kate was serving a client, a woman dressed in a very theatrical getup, when the little bell over the door chimed. She looked at the door to see Alice, who came into the shop swinging her bag on a finger.

Kate glanced at her watch. It was almost ten. She smiled at Alice and continued to show the amber jewelry to the woman with the flowing kaftan, asking herself, and not for the first time, who wore a kaftan in the middle of summer.

Kate wished the woman had decided already so she could go in the back and talk to Alice. Now that she'd made her choice, she was anxious to move on with her plan.

Finally, the client decided on a set sporting a necklace, a bracelet and earrings. Relieved, Kate rang the charge on the woman's credit card and showed her out the door. After the woman disappeared in the crowd, Kate turned the sign on the door to let any potential clients know she would be back in ten minutes and went in the back to talk to Alice.

"Oh, hi, Kate. Has the client left?" Alice turned to Kate, all the while doctoring a cup of coffee with cream and sugar.

"Yes, Alice, she did. I just wanted to talk to you for a few minutes before you go on the floor," Kate said, waving Alice to a seat in front of her office desk.

"Yes, of course. Is everything all right?" Alice asked and sat down.

She took care to smoothen her skirt over her legs and Kate smiled. Alice had her idiosyncrasies but she liked her for that.

"Oh, yes, don't worry, Alice. Everything's fine. Do you remember we spoke about me taking a vacation?" Kate started, tentatively.

"Yes, of course, I remember just fine. I still think it would do you good to leave Montreal for a while. And I mean for more than three or four days. Have you thought about it?" Alice asked and tasted her coffee to see if it was the way she liked it.

"Well, yes," Kate replied.

She decided not to tell Alice all the story. She disliked skirting around the truth but she thought it was better if Alice didn't know what she planned.

"You see… I seem to have a chance to leave for about three weeks… I'd be going to Malaysia with some friends for a vacation…," Kate said.

She didn't look directly at Alice. She knew she wasn't very good at lying. Her face betrayed her all the time.

"That's great, Kate," Alice rejoiced hearing her plan.

"Well, yes, it is, but I should be leaving tonight at around eleven o'clock, I'm afraid. I know it's quite sudden and that gives you very short notice about the change in your schedule…"

"Don't worry about that, Kate, just go," Alice waved her concerns away. "I'll work a split shift, so I could open the shop in the morning and close it in the evening, and Jeanne can work the hours in between. She's off school, with it being summer, and just yesterday she told me she could use some more hours right now. You know young girls and summer time...," she winked. "So, it's just perfect, you see. It works just fine if she can work eight hours a day, you know? Of course, our shift will overlap somewhere in the middle, but I think it'll be fine... So, you see, you can leave anytime. You should even go home and get ready now. Everything is covered here, I promise you," Alice said.

"So, you wouldn't mind," Kate surmised. She was amused with Alice's enthusiasm.

"No, of course not, just the opposite. I've been thinking about this for a while now. You need a longer vacation. You deserve it, girl, and you know it. You've been working your ass off for a long time and you haven't taken care of you at all. I'll take care of things here, so, just go," Alice said smiling, and she jumped up, ready to show Kate out the door.

Kate burst into laughter and said, "All right, I'm going, I'm going. No need to throw me out of the door." Then, in a serious voice, she explained, "You're the boss for the next three weeks, Alice. I'll prepare the checks for your pays, including the eight hours per day for

Jeanne. You will get a raise and a bonus because you'll be working more, okay? You'll have to receive the orders and pay for them ... I'll leave the checks for that as well. Of course, you'll have to give Jeanne her paycheck. All those checks will be in this drawer here," Kate showed Alice the right top drawer of her desk.

"I wouldn't say '*no*' to more money, Kate, you know me," Alice laughed and stood up.

She took her coffee cup with her and went into the shop to turn the sign on the door back to open.

\*\*\*

Kate wrote the checks for the three pays she would be missing and verified the stock once more to make sure she had all the orders put in. She also verified the checks for the suppliers' payments. Alice needed only to pick up a check and pay a supplier.

After she finished organizing everything, she reserved a return ticket for her flight to Malaysia at eleven that evening, and because the plane landed at around ten in the morning, she booked one night at the same hotel where she was supposed to leave the money.

She didn't imagine Ryan would guess she was the messenger. She wanted to have a glimpse of him at least. After all, the man had bothered her for several months already and she couldn't just write those months off.

In the spur of the moment, she also made a reservation and paid for a vacation house on the beach. If she had to fly all that way to Malaysia, and it was a very long way, indeed, at least she could enjoy three weeks in the sun.

Kate spent about twelve thousand dollars, and when she totalled all the expenses, she sighed. She comforted herself with the thought she was compensating for the six years when she hadn't gone anywhere.

She checked everything again to be sure that things were in order and when everything checked out, she went into the shop and called Alice to come into her crammed office and go over the papers with her.

Jeanne had already started her shift and Kate knew she could take care of the customers for a while. Meanwhile, Kate had to make sure Alice was trained in everything there was to be known about managing the shop for the following three weeks.

***

When she was confident Alice understood everything and could look after the business during her three-week vacation, Kate left the shop and went to the bank to withdraw ten thousand dollars from her bank account. She was a careful person, who planned for all contingencies, so, she also checked whether she could use her debit card and credit card abroad or if she had to rely on traveller's checks.

After her brief stop at the bank, where everything went smoothly and the news was quite reassuring, she went to *The Bay* to buy a small bag for Ryan's nine thousand dollars. She carefully chose a bag any man would carry without objection.

Kate thought about her wardrobe and sighed. She had to spend more money now. She needed a few clothes for her summer experience, somewhat different from her everyday getup.

After she gave it a bit of thought, she decided she had to add something that would help her to be unrecognizable. She wanted to get a look at Ryan when he would come to take the money but she didn't want him to recognize her.

She completed the ensemble with a chic hat. The wide brim and some huge sunglasses covered almost half of her face. Kate didn't recognize herself when she looked in the mirror.

She added a few books to the things she intended to take with her. If she were to spend three weeks alone on the beach, she needed something to read.

When she finished shopping, Kate stopped by her telephone provider's store and arranged for roaming. She also verified whether she could access the Internet on her tablet while away.

# CHAPTER TEN

*A day and a half earlier at around 11 pm – July 17th*

Five minutes after eleven p.m., the plane took off for Turkey, the first leg of her flight. On board, Kate wondered for the tenth time what the hell she'd been thinking to fly halfway around the world in the spur of the moment. It was a very long flight even with the layover in Istanbul.

Kate had already sent a message to Ryan to let him know he could find the money at the front desk of the hotel at four in the afternoon the following day. She'd reserved enough time to get from the airport to the hotel and to rest for a while. She'd also cautiously banked some time in case of any delays during her trip.

Kate read Ryan's enthusiastic reply but she didn't answer the phone when he called. She refused to have any contact with him for the next twenty-four hours.

The flight attendant came with dinner on a tray after the plane reached cruising altitude and Kate dubiously eyed her plate. It didn't seem very appetizing and as she had already eaten before leaving home, she left the tray aside and went to sleep.

She would be in Istanbul after nine hours and forty minutes. That was enough time for a good night's sleep.

\*\*\*

Kate woke up an hour before landing. The flight attendants had already started to serve breakfast and, this time, she accepted the tray, and asked for some coffee. She ate her pastries, lazily listening to the chatter around her.

She'd been lucky. The seat next to her had remained unoccupied and no one disturbed her. She'd even used both seats to sleep and felt somewhat refreshed.

Kate drank her coffee and peered through the window. She tried not to think about the second leg of the trip and especially, not about the moment when her eyes would finally lie on Ryan.

She had two hours and fifty-five minutes to kill in Istanbul and another eleven hours to get to Kuala Lumpur. She had enough time to ponder upon what was to come. For the moment, she chose to let her mind wander.

\*\*\*

Kate deplaned in Istanbul and went to the passport control point. A polite officer directed her to the Primeclass Lounge, one floor below the Food Court, after the control point.

When she entered the lounge, she found herself immersed in a world she hadn't ever imagined. For a young woman who'd spent her life between studies and work, and who hadn't left Montreal in over a decade, the lounge looked like a different world.

Kate spent an hour and a half tasting the delicacies displayed and taking it all in. The cultural differences seemed overwhelming at times but she imbibed herself in all that novelty with a passion.

When the time to embark came, she regretted to leave the lounge. The novelty helped her forget about what waited for her at the end of the flight.

Kate dreaded the flight to Malaysia. The flight took almost eleven hours and only thinking of that she felt exhausted.

Kate congratulated herself she'd asked Ryan to come and take the money in the afternoon. That way, she could rest and refresh. She could also arrange everything with the clerk at the front desk.

She hoped the receptionist would be open to her plan. Otherwise she didn't know how she would recognize Ryan when he came to take the money.

Of course, if he would be the one coming to take the money. Her research showed that entire networks operated out there. The person coming to get the money could be anyone.

The thought of Ryan being part of a scam operation distressed her. She almost hated herself for letting him worm his way into her heart. She half suspected everything was just part of a very well strategized operation and she was just a mark.

Well, in the end, everyone had to make some big mistakes in their life, and she hadn't made any before. Probably, it was her turn

She could live with that. She would probably think about it now and then and feel ashamed she'd fallen for it, but at least she'd tried her luck.

Once on the plane, she waited for takeoff, and then, she curled in her chair and slept some more. She was lucky again. No one occupied the seat next to hers.

She didn't care about dinner and let the flight attendant know she shouldn't bother with her food. She requested not to be disturbed and, once she closed her eyes, she was fast asleep.

\*\*\*

The morning sun woke Kate. She was confused about her whereabouts. She blinked a few times and then she remembered where she was and why.

She looked around. Most people were still sleeping. Quietly, she went to the lavatory to clean herself as much as possible. When she came back, the cabin attendants had already started to serve breakfast and a tray had been left in front of her seat.

After she started to eat, the flight attendant came and offered her coffee or tea. Kate felt exhausted despite the long hours of sleep and needed some coffee to start up her day.

The trip took a toll on her. She felt the strain of the journey and she still had another two hours and a half before landing. When she thought of the forty-five-minute drive from the airport to the Majestic hotel, she sighed.

Her reflection in the lavatory mirror had dismayed Kate. She looked pale and had dark circles around her eyes.

She promised herself never to travel for almost twenty-four uninterrupted hours. It was pure madness.

Kate hoped the four hours she had before Ryan came would be enough for her to feel somewhat refreshed and, more importantly, to look better and not like death warmed over.

Kate sipped her coffee broodingly, looking at the clouds below, and as she was prone to do, she played different scenarios in her mind.

She had some control over the evolution of things and that satisfied her. She had determined how the *'business'* should be concluded. She refused to call that stage in her relationship with Ryan otherwise. She was determined to avoid being swept into a melodrama.

Kate felt bitter. She believed it was natural to feel regret, although she'd never counted on anything real coming out of the story with Ryan.

Yet, she'd felt close to Ryan. The man always perceived the funny side of things and she'd been attracted to his acerb wit and varied knowledge. They would talk about books and films and even philosophy.

Ryan had proved complicated and well read. She hadn't thought a scammer would be so versed in the art of conversation.

More than that, she'd been attracted to him, the man, and she hadn't even met him yet. That simply boggled her mind. She couldn't understand how she could react so strongly to a man she'd never seen.

Kate reckoned she'd have liked a true relationship with Ryan. She'd enjoyed even their sparring and laughter over menial things.

Now, she feared she'd built that relationship entirely in her imagination. She also dreaded she'd never find something like that again in real life. Probably, a few years down the road, she would settle for less and she hated that thought.

The captain's voice interrupted her reflections, prompting the passengers to fasten their seatbelts. The procedures for landing had started and Kate was anxious to see what the next few hours would bring. The thought of laying eyes on Ryan was terrifying and exhilarating at the same time.

With new determination, she deplaned and, after passing through the passport control point, she went to the car rental office to pick up the keys for the car she'd booked from Montreal.

After signing the papers for a small convertible, she began her forty-five-minute drive toward the Majestic and possibly, toward Ryan.

Kate didn't even take the time to admire the surrounding landscape. She knew she would have all the time in the world during the following three weeks. She'd enjoy the atmosphere and life in

Malaysia then. For the moment, she was a woman on a mission.

***

At the hotel, after taking her only luggage bag from the back seat, Kate handed the car keys to the valet. She smiled at the doorman and, going inside, she made a beeline to the front desk, manned by a young smiling man.

# CHAPTER ELEVEN

*Back to present day – July 19$^{th}$*

The man didn't answer anything for a while and the silence grew menacing.

"Are you still there?" she asked when the silence began to weigh heavily on her.

"Yes, I am. I'm here, Kate. And when I say here, that means *here*," his reply came heatedly.

Not a second later, heavy footsteps sounded on the veranda surrounding the house. Startled, Kate looked there and saw him.

He came into view with a scowl tugging at the corner of his lips. He turned off his phone, staring her down. The expression on his face didn't promise anything good.

Kate's legs fell off the other chair with a resonant clank and she froze in place. She even forgot to turn off her phone. By rote, she managed to let it fall on the table in a slow move.

Her eyes turned into two, wide, frozen, green pools of shimmering water. She stared at him.

The man towered over her in an extremely foreboding manner. He looked like he was ready to pounce on her any second now.

Kate was aware of only one thing. She had one very huge pissed-off male looming over her. Any coherent thought vanished. His figure was the focal point.

At the sight of his threatening stance, her throat constricted and she had to make serious efforts just to breathe.

*'Oh, God, the man's so big!'* From a distance, at the hotel, he hadn't seemed so tall or so well-built. Now, Kate realized he had to be about six feet four at least.

Sometime in his past, he'd probably played football for a few years, given his massive muscles. His shirt couldn't even begin to hide them.

He'd clenched his fists so tight that his knuckles turned white. He was tense. The coiled muscles in his arms played under his skin. He looked like he was trying hard to keep his temper in check.

Ryan's dark eyes shone with pure thundering fury and his mouth was drawn in a tight line, making the rest of his face seem rigid and unforgiving. At least, he was trying not to shout or strangle her, although he seemed like he wanted to.

One moment she was sitting and staring stunned at him, a little afraid of his brutal display of force. The next, he reached for her and pulled her up like a rag doll. He shook her so violently that her teeth clattered.

"You stupid, stupid, little girl," Ryan practically growled the words through his teeth, as if it he couldn't unclench his mouth and speak normally.

Witnessing such intense and hot fury, Kate thought that was the end for her. Certainly, she'd be lying dead right there, in a second. She knew she couldn't fight his obvious brutal force.

What followed bewildered her even more. After a few tense moments, during which he continued to shake her so badly that she could feel her bones rattle, he suddenly pulled her close and pressed her to him, holding her in a smothering bear hug. That gesture confused her more.

He buried his face in her hair and inhaled her scent greedily. He looked like a man trying to draw in his next breath with everything he got.

Once her body touched his, Kate felt he was shaking. Nothing made sense to her anymore. She'd probably fallen through the looking glass into a parallel world.

Kate's ears caught his unintelligible whispers. He was whispering something to her, feverishly, but his face was buried in her hair, and she couldn't understand any of the words. Besides, she was still stunned by his reactions and had difficulties in processing anything. She'd expected something else when he'd showed up so mad with her.

Altogether, everything seemed exceedingly unreal. For an instant, she thought she was experiencing all those weird things because of the long flight, which had fried her brain connections.

Kate wasn't aware Ryan followed her to the house from the hotel. Subsequently, his presence on her deck had turned her brains to mush.

His presences there wasn't part of her plan and she feared she'd lost total control of the situation. The only words in her mind were interjections like *'wow'* and *'oh, my God!'* She couldn't articulate any coherent phrases.

Kate tried to pull herself together. She needed to form some coherent ideas.

Her reasoning power had disappeared the moment she saw Ryan from up close. He was much more than she'd imagined.

His physique astounded her. Kate had never been the type of woman to sigh or faint over big muscles and a broad chest. She'd preferred the intellectual type.

Now, the reality proved she'd been lying to herself. Ryan's body had basically robbed her mind of any rational thought. She felt a bit ashamed of such a girly reaction. She hadn't ever reacted that way. Not even when she was a teenager.

Kate had never expected to see a man so entranced by holding her. He couldn't form any comprehensible sentences. Oddness notwithstanding, his reaction delighted Kate once she became aware she had such power over him.

That time around she was positive he couldn't just play a part to mislead her. He couldn't be such a good actor.

"Ryan," she managed to mumble. Her face was still buried in his chest. Every breath brought the smell of his slightly sweaty skin and played havoc with her senses.

Ryan didn't answer, as if he hadn't heard her. The man held her tight against his body with his left arm, all the while trailing the contour of her face with the callous fingers of his other hand. His raspy touch left a pleasantly burning sensation in its wake and made her experience that strange tingling in her lower belly once again.

His lips brushed the ridges of her ear and the featherlike touch prompted her to shiver slightly. Now, that strange tingling was present everywhere, all over her body and inside her body. It brought a myriad of unknown but painfully pleasant sensations to life. All of them exploded inside her and made her blood sing.

"Ryan," she said more forcefully.

Kate needed to get back to normal and get out of that trance of senses. This time, she met with some success in her attempt to bring him back to reality.

"What?" Ryan mumbled slightly annoyed for being interrupted.

He didn't stop though. He continued to trace the contour of her cheekbone with his fingers and his slightly open and wet lips followed closely.

Kate laughed softly at his annoyance, and that surprised her. After a few seconds, she remembered what she wanted and said, "I do think that we should talk first, Ryan, don't you?"

Kate's voice hesitated. She didn't know for sure whether she wanted that sweet torture to end.

For the first time in her lifetime, she believed talking was overrated. Allowing her body to experience something so electrifying couldn't be wrong.

"What's there to talk about?" Ryan asked gruffly, pulling slightly away and looking straight into her eyes with annoyance. "You're here, although we both know you shouldn't be...," he frowned, but continued, "I'm here... and I need you, baby, really, really bad, and right now. No more postponing, no more waiting...I can't wait anymore. I've been thinking of this too much and..."

"We've just met, Ryan," Kate interrupted him in a dry voice.

She tried to be logical and help him see reason at the same time, although it wasn't easy for her to be rational when her skin was burning.

"But we know each other well enough, Kate. Come on. We've known each other long enough, don't you think? We've talked and argued for so many hours that... No, no more talking or arguing would bring us closer than this, Kate... Don't you see I'm right, baby? Please, think, or better don't think," he almost implored her and then brushed a lock of her hair aside to get to the curve of her cheek, which he cradled tenderly in his palm.

He tilted his head forward, his eyes intently on hers, ready to notice the slightest glimmer and reaction. He brushed her lips with his lightly, enticing her to accept the inevitable and give in.

Kate stared at him for a few seconds. Then, she had to reckon she wasn't able to refuse his request. She couldn't say *'no'* to him. And besides, if she wanted to be completely truthful with herself, she had to admit she didn't have any intention to refuse his advances. Her entire body already vibrated in tune with his. Now, she longed for far more than his light touches.

They didn't truly know each other, if she wanted to be technical. Yet, that could have been true even if they'd met constantly and had all those conversations face to face.

Kate still didn't know who he was. She had no idea whether he was a scammer or not, but she didn't want to think about that anymore and, more specifically, not when he held her in his arms as if she'd been something very precious to him.

She was there and he was there and that was all that mattered. She wasn't a risk taker, but that was one of those moments in life when it seemed like it was worth jumping into the unknown with open eyes.

Staring straight into his eyes, to gauge his reactions, Kate reached out and touched his chest timidly. She tried to find her bearings in making love to him. She had limited experience and she'd never taken the initiative before. Kate needed to find her rhythm. After stroking his chest with featherlike touches, her hands slid down his torso slowly, stroked his midriff with by now shaky hands, and then stole behind his back.

His pupils were getting more dilated and intense, and she surmised he enjoyed her touches probably as much as she enjoyed having her hands on him. She melted into him. She aligned her torso to his so she could feel much more of his body.

Her moist lips found his collarbone and she left a trail of wet kisses on his feverish, dark skin, tasting his musky and manly flavor. She traced a swirling path from one side to the other of his collarbone with the tip of her tongue and relished in the salty taste his skin left on her tongue. At the same time, her fingers burrowed into the hard muscles of his back, massaging lightly at first. Then she alternated light touches with deep ones. His muscles flexed and shivered under her playful fingers and a short victorious laughter flew off her lips.

The sound of her laughter surprised Ryan and he arched his left eyebrow. Kate was also astonished how much she liked feeling his body without any restrictions and playing it like a violin.

Ryan's eyes, even half-lidded, were still keenly focused on her. The suspense and his expectations had dried his lips and he licked his upper lip briefly. He inhaled sharply when she reached up and the tip of her tongue licked the hollow at the base of his neck in a whorl.

"Enough teasing, baby," he grumbled.

His voice was tense and hoarse. He whisked her up into his arms and made her cry out in surprise. She threw her arms around his neck for support, afraid that he would drop her any moment now.

Watching Kate's face intently, he started toward the house with big and hurried steps. She felt he was in a rush to find her bedroom immediately and start feasting on her. That image made her both blush and shiver, which prompted Ryan to grin like a wolf and his innate primitive streak became more vivid in his eyes. It promised a lot more was about to come. For a moment, Kate was afraid the intensity of what would follow might consume her.

Kate had never believed she would enjoy being carried away like that or she would be pleased to have fueled such raw masculinity in a man. As a rule, she'd run away from that type of man. Prudence didn't go hand in hand with raw emotions.

Kate enjoyed deeply Ryan's arrogance and his intense demonstration of sheer physical power.

Instinctively, Ryan chose the correct path to her bedroom and carried her inside the room after only a few huge strides. There, he let her slide slowly along his body until her feet touched the floor.

He loved how she felt against him and how his skin burnt at the direct contact with the woman's body. He didn't let her go. He kept her close for a few more seconds, his eyes searching hers as deep as possible. He wanted to make sure she was on the same page with him and wanted the intimacy they shared as much as he did.

Once he was assured he didn't misunderstand her, he pushed himself to arm's length and allowed his eyes to roam freely all over her body, from head to toes. An appreciative and hungry grin appeared on his lips and assured her he was pleased with everything he saw.

The man reached behind her and found the zipper of her dress. Excruciatingly slowly, and the anticipation almost killed her, he lowered it and followed the progress with his eyes. The dress came loose around Kate's breasts and now he could relish in a little more than a hint of her bosom. The rosy skin beaconed to him and he didn't bother to fight his desire. Ryan carefully traced the contour of one breast, directly on her skin, with one of his fingers.

Kate's eyes didn't leave him. He focused intensely on what his finger was doing. His eyes never strayed from the path his callous finger was following, as if the texture of her skin had fascinated him.

Her body captivated his eyes. His rough skin left goose bumps on her body in its wake. When she slightly trembled, Ryan suddenly looked up and noticed her pupils had widened and her lips had parted, inviting him to taste them.

Ryan had already decided not to refuse her or himself anything, so he leaned forward, licked his lips nervously, and then touched them to hers. He caught her light exhale in his mouth, and answered back with a deep growl of his own.

That profound rumble reminded Kate of ancient times. That was how her fancy nature had imagined the warriors of the past, raw and ravenous.

Ryan brushed his lips to hers a couple of times. He tested them, trying to learn their texture and shape. Only afterwards, his tongue dove into her mouth, and tasted her. He teased Kate mercilessly. His tongue danced slowly over hers, mating with her.

By now, he had already closed his fingers over one of her breasts and pressed the little bud with the centre of his palm. He liked how it felt when the little peak bumped into his hand. He stroked it with his knuckles and then squeezed it gently between two fingers at first, and then more strongly. When he rolled her nipple between his fingers, Kate inhaled sharply and her arms stole around his neck, looking for support. That made him wallow in his power. Knowing she needed an anchor because her legs shook, made him feel close to invincible. At the same time, he inhaled her scent and allowed the taste of her tongue explode onto his, which brought him almost to the brink.

Ryan loved the way she responded to his mating ritual. Her answer was unconscious. She allowed her tongue blend with his and matched her moves to his.

Kate's fingers knotted in his hair. She didn't care if he hurt or not. Ryan didn't care either. He just wanted to make her experience so many sensations at the same time, so they would wreak havoc on her brain and body.

Ryan suddenly pulled back again and glanced with proud at her swollen lips. He had done that to her.

The man grinned mischievously at her, as if he had plans for something more. Then, he drew her toward him again. Their bodies bumped one into the other, and Ryan took her mouth in a mind-numbing kiss. He then stroked her lips with his tongue and nipped at her lower lip sharply, which made her cry out and pull his hair in response.

He merely chuckled. It was that throaty laughter of his that made her always shiver.

Then, he turned his attention back to feasting on her mouth and tried to become one with her. His skilled tongue played on hers, stroking and teasing, brushing slowly on her teeth and her lips at times.

Ryan pulled back only when his body screamed for air and he exploded with too much need for air. His blood roared in his ears, covering even the sound of the waves coming through the window Kate had left open earlier.

"I love your dress, baby," he said through clenched teeth, "It suits you… But let's get rid of it, okay? I need to touch you everywhere," Ryan fervently whispered to her. His patience was frizzled, hanging on a thread.

Kate was so dizzy she couldn't make sense of his words. She glanced at him confused and that made him laugh again, pleased with himself.

"The dress, baby. Let's take it off," Ryan repeated louder.

To make her move, he decided to lead through example. He reached back and pulled his shirt over his head, throwing it somewhere in the room.

When she saw him taking his clothes off, Kate finally understood what he wanted from her and she pushed the straps of her summer dress off her shoulders. She let the dress pool at her feet. The texture of the cotton sliding over her feverish body cooled her skin.

The woman needed that respite from the fuzzy world in which Ryan had pushed her with his lips and fingers.

Kate stood in front of him clad in her skimpy panties and her bra. When she noticed the hungry look in his eyes and the way his eyes roamed over her body thoroughly, she blushed violently. Ryan seemed to memorize everything.

The man didn't miss the blush spread all over her face and neck, and beamed in response. He took his shoes off and told her, "Few women know how to blush properly after puberty. I love it on you, Kate."

She wanted to reply something witty but, surprisingly, her mind didn't hold a thought. She shrugged. She'd never been good at sexual banter anyway. She'd become aware flirting wasn't part of her genetic makeup long before her teenage period ended and she'd accepted her shortcomings without complaints.

"You'd like me to take off the rest, wouldn't you?" Ryan inquired naughtily.

He'd already thrown his shoes away and unzipped his jeans. His eyes fixed on Kate, he took his jeans off together with his underwear and Kate's wide eyes stared at him. Her reaction brought another satisfied grin on Ryan's lips. All her responses flattered Ryan and made him more confident in his skills.

After a few seconds, Kate shook her head and reached back to unhook her bra, but Ryan stopped her.

"No, babe, allow me. I'd love to unwrap you. You're my gift right now."

Reticently, her arms fell aside and he reached behind her, his eyes always on hers. He unhooked her bra and pulled the straps down, freeing her breasts. Throwing the bra on the floor carelessly, Ryan closed his palms over the two mounds and massaged them lightly, growling possessively again. That growl and his touches were enough to make her blood boil again.

When his palms closed on her, Kate staggered and grasped his arms to find her balance. Her nails dug into his skin but she didn't care about his pain.

He lowered his head and brought her left breast to his mouth. His tongue licked the underside of her breast, tasting the salty skin, breathing her in. At the same time, he slid his fingers all over her right breast and rejoiced when he felt her shaking under his touch. When his fingers finally reached the tightened nipple, his mouth closed simultaneously on the other one. His tongue swirled around it and made it harder, just perfect for him to suck on.

Kate cried out. Too many sensations, all of them extremely intense, shot through her. Tension surged in every fiber of her body. Her preservation sense demanded she pulled back, but his arm stole behind her and held her fast in place.

Ryan didn't leave any room for her to move, and all the while he continued to feast on her hungrily. He licked her nipple, molding it with his tongue and then, suddenly, he sharply nipped at it with his teeth. Kate exhaled shakily. Ryan sucked the little bud, until he felt the tension exploding in her body and she dissolved in a sea of sensations. Ryan didn't stop until Kate began to shake and whimper in his arms.

He glanced at her face. Her eyes were closed and her lips, wearing the mark of her own teeth, had parted in a mute shout. That urged him to reach up to her full mouth. He followed her suit and bit her lower lip sharply, making her cry out again.

Kate tilted toward him blindly. She needed support and she rested her head onto his shoulder in complete abandon.

Ryan nudged her head up with his thumb and, to her surprise, the man maliciously bit her lower lip once more. That prompted her to cling onto his shoulders with shaking fingers.

Feeling her tremble, he took the time to assuage her tormented reddened lip with wet and soft touches before sucking it into his mouth. He growled when he filled himself with her texture, taste and smell. He sucked on the plump lip, something he'd been craving since he saw her photo.

Nothing else existed for him. Ryan didn't perceive the murmur of the sea or the smell of salt lingering in the air. He was just breathing and feeling Kate and that was it for him.

After something that felt like a small eternity, his lips started their journey away from her mouth, and stroked her jaw, tracing the shape of her cheekbone. Then, he kissed one eyelid and then the other.

His featherlike touches descended then on the other side of Kate's face. Ryan licked the whorl of her ear lazily, and then, he sank his teeth in her earlobe softly. Kate gasped and her fingers burrowed into his shoulders, her nails leaving marks behind. He continued to pepper little kisses on her neck here and there, until he reached the point where her neck melted into her shoulder blade and, there, he sucked strongly, alternating the suckling with elusive licking and bites, savouring all the while the passionate sounds coming from Kate's lips.

Kate had lost any lucid thought and her brain knew only one thing. She needed Ryan and she needed him right then. She'd had enough foreplay. She felt like she would have died if he hadn't furthered their lovemaking faster. Kate was set on fire. She burnt everywhere.

Ryan read her thoughts in her eyes. He grinned at her and shook his head. He wanted her to understand he was the one in control of their lovemaking and she had to respect his timetable.

Then, he slightly bent and his fingers delved into her panties. He pulled them excruciatingly slowly down her legs, and his knuckles stroked the length of each leg all the way down, leaving a trail of goosebumps in their wake.

Once he removed her panties and thrown them away, Ryan kneeled before her and pulled her to him, to bury his mouth in her belly button, where he allowed his tongue to play and tease while his fingers burrowed in her hips. He knew he was marking her and she would show bruises on her hips the following day.

At the thought he was marking her, he became much more territorial and possessive, as if some latent Neanderthal genes had taken control of his mind. He couldn't look beyond the feeling that she belonged to him at visceral level.

He continued to stroke her body with his mouth in his way downward. The soft skin stretched on her hipbone, as well as her spicy smell, fascinated him.

Ryan's senses were raw and his body screamed for completion. He needed to bury himself inside her and forget about everything else.

Ryan stood up and kissed her briefly, almost perfunctorily, and then, he lifted her into his arms and laid her down on the bed. He followed and covered her with his body. He tried to stroke the inside of her thighs some more but his hands were shaking violently.

He couldn't wait another moment. More roughly than he'd wanted to, he delved inside her, filling and stretching her beyond what she'd have thought possible. She cried out at the shock and he hissed through his clenched teeth.

"Did I hurt you, baby?" Ryan asked after a moment, although the effort required a lot from him.

Kate felt too good and he wouldn't have stopped making love to her for nothing in the world.

"No, I was just surprised," Kate replied in a whisper and her right palm stroked the side of his face, reassuring him and encouraging him to continue.

Yet, even through the haze of his pleasure, he noticed tears in her eyes and cringed. "I hurt you, you're crying," he said with dismay.

"Oh, no, no, I'm not crying, Ryan. I was just surprised... pleasantly surprised, actually," she rushed to say, afraid that he would leave her aroused like that. Her body was demanding fulfillment.

"It feels good, doesn't it?" he grinned at her then.

Ryan braced on his elbows and cradled her head in his palms. He kissed her softly with tenderness.

"It does Ryan, but if you don't start to move...," Kate replied in a threatening voice and pushed her pelvis up toward him.

Ryan laughed and arched forcefully into her, making her gasp again. He began making passionate love to her and lavished her lips with wet and demanding kisses. His chest brushed hers every time they came together and both felt electrifying shocks in their nerve endings. He pulled her left leg around his waist and pushed harder inside her, and at the same time, he stroked her thigh with the tips of his fingers. He enjoyed feeling her quivering violently.

Ryan's arousal increased when her shaky fingers caressed his back. The idea of being inside her and being surrounded by her like a tight glove excited him even more.

He'd have liked to kiss her again but realized he couldn't. His mouth had tightened because he tried to last longer.

Her smell intoxicated his senses and he knew he would be done soon. He reached down, stroked her womanhood and buried himself in her deeper. Ryan caressed her body with his at every move, and finally, she uncoiled. The tension inside her was released in a powerful wave of pleasure.

Kate gasped and then, cried out. Her eyes opened wide. They were trained on him, full of astonishment. What she felt was much more than she'd expected.

Only then, satisfied that she'd reached fulfillment, Ryan also let go. He roared into her neck and collapsed on top of her, but immediately turned on his side and took her with him so he wouldn't crush her with his weight. Then he felt wetness on his thigh and looked down in alarm. Stunned, he discovered he'd forgotten something essential.

"I didn't use anything. Damn it! Of course, I didn't. Bloody hell, I didn't have anything to use. Oh, damn it!" he cursed a string, disgusted with himself.

Kate stared at him nonplussed for a few seconds. She didn't understand what had come over him. Then, the truth dawned on her and she replied, "I'm on the pill, no worries there. I'm healthy..."

"So, am I, baby, don't worry about that. I was concerned only about a pregnancy. We've never talked about that and..."

Kate didn't reply. She just shrugged, and laid her head back on his shoulder. She was too exhausted to discuss anything anymore. She needed to sleep.

Ryan looked at the top of her head with indecision. He'd have liked to clear matters with her right then, but he gave up when he saw she wasn't ready for that conversation.

He kissed her hair, and gathered her in his arms, as tightly as possible, and said, "Rest for a few moments, sweetie. Later, we'll have to talk though."

She didn't answer back, as she'd already fallen asleep. The gruelling trip, the anticipation of spying on Ryan, the shock of having him in her vacation house, but most of all, the most intense lovemaking she'd ever experienced, had worn her out.

Ryan looked at her and grinned with pure male satisfaction. After a few seconds, though, he frowned. There were still far too many things that needed an answer. Yet, he had to wait for her to wake up so, he settled her better in his arms, and watched over her sleep.

# CHAPTER TWELVE

When she woke up, Kate found herself alone in bed, covered with a silky sheet up to her shoulders. Her body felt strange and when she looked down she saw the traces left by Ryan's beard and his demanding fingers. She wore his prints on her hips and she was shocked to realize she'd allowed a man to mark her.

Kate got out of bed and scowled at her muscles' loud protest. She'd never been so thoroughly loved and used before and her body complained.

She went to the bathroom and looked at herself in the mirror. Her hair looked mussed up. Her swollen and bruised lips reminded her of Ryan's clever mouth, and she tingled all over again.

She glanced back at the bed she'd shared with Ryan and shook her head. She couldn't believe it. She had jumped into the bed with a man after only a matter of minutes.

In the shower, she let the water soothe her aching body first. She kept thinking of Ryan and the surreal afternoon she'd spent with him. Kate believed he'd already left and sorrow filled her heart.

She'd been assured she would find strict necessities in the fridge and went to grab a bite. She was sad but the vigorous lovemaking had left her famished.

Ryan's presence in the kitchen shocked her. He was making an omelette and talking on the phone at the same time.

"So, Adam's the same not worse," he said and then, as if he'd felt she'd entered the room, he glanced at her.

Kate stopped right on the threshold. She didn't trust either him or herself if she came inside the kitchen.

Ryan smiled at her but his smile didn't reach his eyes, which shone with cold detachment. He continued his phone conversation, as if her arrival didn't matter.

Kate resented his attitude and for a moment, she thought of going back to bed. Her hesitation lasted one second, though. She changed her mind and advanced into the kitchen. That was her vacation house, after all, and she refused to let him take control over the house or her actions.

"Well, Nick, I'll see what's what and depending on what I find out, we might have to move again. Call you back," Ryan said and hung up.

He replaced the phone back into his pocket carefully. Then, he turned to the stove and flipped the omelette.

"So, you're finally up," he observed in a cold voice, without turning to her.

"Yes, I am," Kate answered softly. She didn't know how to react in front of this new Ryan.

She'd got used to the temperamental Ryan and the man in front of her eyes was completely different.

"I was very tired, of course, what, after that long flight and then the wait at the hotel..." she continued and stopped when she realized she was rambling.

"Oh, yeah, the wait at the hotel, indeed," he replied maliciously. "We need to talk about that now, don't we?"

Kate shrugged non-committedly and sat at the table. She knew he would bring the subject up sooner or later when she found him in the kitchen. She didn't care for it but doubted she had a choice.

"I see you're cooking," she said just to fill in the silence. "Is there something in there for me too?"

"Of course, there is," Ryan replied. "I started cooking when I heard you move around the bedroom. I hope you like Spanish omelette. For anything else, we need to make a trip to the shop," he joked lightly.

"I thought of doing that tomorrow. I hoped I would find enough food in there for tonight," Kate replied pointing to the fridge. "I didn't have time to check, you know…" she stopped slightly embarrassed when she remembered what sidetracked her.

Ryan came to the table, leaned over her and asked in a very serious voice, "Any regrets, Kate?"

Kate looked straight into his eyes. To her surprise, he showed concern. She hadn't expected it from him and she tried to probe his mind once more, only to feel him pushing her away. She noticed he frowned and looked at her inquiringly. Yet, he said nothing.

She didn't know how it was possible but he seemed to feel her probing his mind. She'd never encountered that before. It befuddled her.

At the beginning, when she discovered her gift, she'd been scared. Thankfully, her grandma was still alive and she explained she had a gift passed down on females in their family, every generation. She advised Kate not to speak of her talent to anyone. People would try to take advantage of her or consider her a freak or worse.

Kate grew up and learned that people had difficulty in accepting someone who was very different. They considered such individuals a threat. She kept her gift secret and not even her best friend, Ellie, knew about it.

Kate suddenly realized Ryan hadn't said anything and glanced at him. He still waited for her to answer to his question and his inquiring eyes pulled her back to the real world.

"No. No regrets, Ryan. Not now and not in the future. That's something I can promise you," Kate finally replied. "I wanted it and I really enjoyed it, as you very well know. So...," she shrugged.

"That's good, baby, because I'm afraid I can't stop now. One taste of you and I've been hooked. No matter why you're here and the consequences of your arrival, I still need to taste you again," he said and brushed a lock of her hair away from her face and behind her ear.

"What do you mean by *'the consequences of my arrival'*?" Kate inquired with a frown.

"All right, we'll do it right now then," Ryan said, nodding.

He stood up and went to take the omelette off the stove. He divided it onto two plates and set a plate and fork in front of her. He went back to the counter for the tomatoes and cucumbers he'd cut on a cutting board earlier. He put them on a plate which he laid in the middle of the table for both to share. With a wide wave, he invited her to eat.

Ryan spooned some eggs and chewed in silence for a few moments. Then, he asked her, "Who sent you here?"

Kate looked up at him confused, "I beg your pardon?"

"Now, don't play coy with me, baby. Who sent you here?" Ryan repeated in a steely voice and continued to eat, watching her intently.

"I don't get it," Kate said. "Who could send me, Ryan? If I remember correctly, I came here to leave the money for you, as we discussed," she explained in a confused voice.

She began to get angry with him. Her voice was strained and a note higher than usual.

"There must be more to that, Kate," the man replied, shaking his head. "No one makes such a long trip, and spends so much money, just to deliver some cash to someone." Ryan argued, always very calm and cold.

Kate didn't recognize that Ryan. She'd expected fury and recriminations because she hadn't told him she was coming to spy on him. Yet, she hadn't expected his cold assessment and dry tone. Both implied he'd already put their recent closeness behind and she didn't like it.

"Well," Kate said and shrugged, "I wanted to see you. I thought I'd be entitled to do so considering how much time I spent talking to you over the last few months and how much money you had requested from me," she argued. "Besides, I hadn't taken a vacation for a few years now, so I decided to combine the two. So, what's the problem?" she leaned forward and almost shouted the question in his face.

"The problem is I don't know if I can trust you," Ryan replied without emotion.

"That's grand," she shouted, losing her calm.

She threw the fork on the table and, suddenly, stood up in a fury. Her chair fell to the floor with a resonant bang.

"That's indeed grand of you, Ryan! *You* can't trust me!"

Kate threw her hands in the air and walked to the window. She took a few deep breaths to calm down.

Ryan didn't show any concern. He continued eating his food, although he still watched her. She was a riddle he needed to solve. Nothing more.

Kate turned back to him, her eyes sparking with thunder. He understood she was mad like a cat and waited for the blows to come.

"What about how much I can trust you? Huh? What about that, Ryan?"

Kate shouted and, with angry strides, she made her way back to the table. She was livid.

"You insinuated your way into my life. Day and night, night and day, you tried to find and push all my buttons. Then, you ask me for so much money that, of course, I had to trust you. How come? If I had asked you something like that, would you have trusted me, Ryan? Think about it. And now, you have the nerve to come here and say you can't trust me. That's just the cherry on top!" Kate shouted once more and tapped the table with her palm.

She went back to the window again and once more, tried to bring her breath back to normal. Watching the waves of the sea or the flow of a river had always helped her.

After a few moments, feeling calm enough, she turned to him and said, "You know what, Ryan? I want you out of here right now and I want you to stay away from me. Don't you ever dare to talk to me or call me. Do you hear me?" she finished her tirade in a banshee-like roar, forgetting about her earlier decision to remain calm.

Ryan coolly nodded and went on with his eating as if nothing had happened.

"Why the hell are you still here? I told you to leave," Kate bellowed to him again.

His indifferent attitude pushed her to lose her temper much more. She felt like slapping him over the head. Yet, the man didn't care she was spitting mad. He just continued eating his food.

Furious because of his dismissal, she went to him and punched him in his shoulder with her fist as hard as she could.

Ryan grinned at her, grasped her fist, opened it and kissed her palm. His tongue swirled around her middle finger, and pulled it in his mouth. He began suckling on it and that made her gasp. All the while, he stared into her eyes.

"Wh... what are you doing?" Kate stuttered and tried to pull her hand away.

"Just kissing your hand, Kate," Ryan replied, and smooched her palm again. Afterwards, he allowed her to pull away.

"You're not in your right mind. That's it. Now, it's clear to me," Kate concluded and pulled away from him, afraid that his mind, which she couldn't read, was twisted.

Ryan laughed cheerfully, finished his food and took his plate to the sink. Then, he turned back to her and said seriously, "I'm in my right mind, baby, no worries. But, I'm in a bend and I was afraid you weren't who you said you were. That was all about," he assured her and his eyes looked very serious.

Kate watched him carefully and asked, "Who did you think I was?"

"Well, when you showed up at the hotel, I thought I'd misjudged you and you lured me into a trap," he confessed.

"But... but... you made love to me," she shouted incredulously.

Kate couldn't believe a man who thought a woman had tried to trap him would sleep with that woman in less than an hour.

"Yes, I did. I couldn't have stopped, Kate. I've been thinking of you for far too long... Your being here didn't help my willpower, you know," Ryan replied bitterly and laughed at himself.

Kate gazed at him for a few moments and then went back to the table. She picked up her fork and started eating, trying to pretend everything was normal. She ate in silence, her eyes always glued on him. Ryan's eyes stared at her, as if he'd tried to decide if his assessment was correct.

"I think," Kate spoke evenly this time "you'd better tell me the whole story, Ryan. I think I'd better know what's going on."

He didn't reply for a few moments. He considered her words first, and then, he returned to the table as well. He sat down and nodded.

"Yes, I think I should tell you the entire story. If nobody had sent you here and you just came to see me, I'll have to make sure you'll be okay. That means you need to know what's going on and from this moment on, you must listen to me and do exactly what I'm saying and when I say it," he said with conviction.

"In your dreams, Ryan," Kate replied haughtily. "I don't take orders from anyone and…"

"You'll take them from me," he interrupted her in an implacable voice. "Your life depends on that, Kate, and you have to get that through your thick skull, do you hear me?"

"More drama?" she mocked him to mask her fear.

"Drama, you say," the man shouted at her. "You, stupid little girl! This is no drama. This is reality, do you understand, Kate? If I must hog-tie you, I'll do it, but you'll listen to me," he repeated and his fist hit the table top with a resonant bang.

Her eyes grew wider when she heard his menacing tone. Her hand shook and she put the fork back on the plate with a loud clank.

"I don't understand why you'd want to scare me like this," Kate said in a small voice.

Despite her early misfortune of losing her parents early in her life, she'd never been in a dangerous situation. Kate was a prudent woman and she'd always avoided the wrong crowd of people. She didn't believe in having an adventure just for the adventure's sake.

"I'm sorry, baby, but it's necessary. I wouldn't do it, but you're in danger now because of your association with me. I've never thought you'd be but then, I didn't know you'd come here yourself, fucking hell. So now, you'll do what you're told, am I clear?" Ryan's voice boomed at the end.

"No, not clear, at all," Kate replied belligerently this time, pushing her chin up in the air. "Either you explain what's what and why or I'll do as I please, and damn your male ego."

"My male ego!!??" Ryan shouted with disbelief. He grabbed her arm and shook her. "You think my ego's the matter, Kate?"

"Manhandling me will not make me cooperate, Ryan," she replied as furious as him. His fingers dug into her arm and his tone didn't sit too well with her.

Ryan stopped shaking her and took a step back. He ran his fingers through his hair in exasperation. He turned away from her and made a few steps while trying to regain his control. He knew it wasn't the right moment to let his temper take the lead in their discussion.

He wasn't proud of the way he'd been handling things with her, especially because he knew he'd hurt her. Yet, he needed to make sure Kate understood what was at stake.

Unfortunately, Ryan had always lacked tactfulness and he needed that now, if he wanted to keep her safe. She was stubborn and wouldn't have listened to him if he'd threatened her.

He faced her again and said, "Have a seat, Kate. I'll tell you everything I can."

"And you'll also tell me how I came into your game, because I'm pretty sure I was just a pawn," she replied spitefully.

He just looked up at her and didn't say anything. After a few moments, he confessed, "Yes, you were… In a way… In the beginning."

Kate didn't have a reply for that, but her eyes threw arrows in his direction. They also revealed her deep hurt. After a couple of seconds, she also sat down, facing him, and waited for him to continue.

"I'll have to start with the beginning, I think, so you can understand my reasons and everything I've done," Ryan said, running his hand through his hair, mussing it up.

Kate nodded and waived her hand, inviting him to continue.

"About half a year ago, one of my best friends, Adam, disappeared here, in Malaysia. In the past, we were a team, a three-man team… We would take impossible missions or missions the government didn't want to touch... They called us when they needed a team of experts to take care of certain... things, let's say. We went together everywhere around the globe, in covert missions, fighting our way in and out of compounds no one could penetrate."

Kate's wide eyes proved her bewilderment. The story captivated her.

A brief smile appeared on his lips and he said, "It was a thrilling period, baby, I admit, but beside the fact we found out what we were made of and of course, made a lot of money in the process, it wasn't a very happy one. Every single day, we had to put our lives on the line and somewhere near the end of our time as a team, things got somehow blurry... We stopped believing in what we were doing... When something like that happens to people like us, it means we lost our focus and could go down at any moment," Ryan said bitterly and his smile turned rueful.

He stopped for a few moments and looked out of the window. In the distance, the sea was glimmering in the sunset, reddish light all over it. It reminded him of Kate's hair and he turned back to her. She waited silently for him to continue.

He inhaled deeply and went on. "Well, the three of us banked the money we made and went our own ways. I know Nick bought a ranch and breeds horses. Adam invested here and there and put the basis of a generous pension plan, and I simply invested half of the money and kept the other half in banks... By now, we could talk about a few millions. Over ten years of very special ops brought us quite a lot of capital...." Ryan paused again and looked away, trying to recollect his thoughts. "Anyway, about half a year ago, the guy who used to direct our missions contacted us for another op. He came to me first... I was the leader and the strategist of the team... Anyway, I flatly turned him down... Don't get me wrong, Kate... I like Mark, or I used to, before all of this happened, but I'd had enough... I thought about starting a business, find me a girl...," Ryan said and grinned at her. "You know, start a family... I'm already thirty-seven, and I'm not getting any younger... I'd like to have children while I can still play football and run around…"

Kate looked at him, checked him up and down, and asked, "Are you really thirty-seven?"

"Actually, I'll be, next month on the 24th," he replied with a smug smile on his lips. He felt proud she found him looking younger.

"Nice, you don't show it. I thought you'd be somewhere near thirty but not over," Kate said giving him another all over.

"Nice to hear it, Kate, but the truth is that I am thirty-seven… That's a fact… I do need to get on with my life… I had about a year after the last mission and I did look around but …. I don't know, women don't seem to be what I hoped for… I had women come onto me when I was working for Mark, and I'd been hoping to find something different… As my luck was… not a chance. It seems I always attract the wrong kind… I started thinking of Internet dating, although I didn't hold too much hope with that either… Anyway, I should get on with the story that brought us both here."

"That would be good," Kate replied and nodded. "I think I have an idea, but I prefer to hear it from you, not to guess."

"Well, as I said, I refused Mark. I told him I was done with all that stuff and he should find someone else. Afterwards, I heard he contacted Nick and Adam, my other two pals, and Nick refused him as well... Adam accepted the mission, though, especially because he was told that the mission was particularly cut for only one person. It wasn't like he had to enter somewhere by force or something like that. He had only to infiltrate a group and report back to Mark. Mark told him not to say a thing to anyone, including to Nick or myself... Secrecy, you know... That son of a bitch didn't even tell Adam we two had already refused the mission," Ryan growled and jumped out of his chair, furious again.

He marched to the window where he stopped. He ran his fingers through his hair one more time.

Kate waited for him to chill out. Her eyes followed his movements through the kitchen. She understood he was feeling powerless. It was obvious he was the type of man who liked control over every situation.

Silence stretched out for a few minutes. Kate watched him flexing his fists. His shoulders tensed. She regretted she couldn't see his face, and especially, his eyes.

Finally, Ryan turned around and looked at her. "In a nutshell, Adam left alone and got into a very bad situation. Someone betrayed him, although we're not sure yet whether the trap was a set up for all of us. When Adam called for our help, and we came, we were expected. We managed to clear Adam out, but he got badly hurt during the fight... We didn't dare to reach out to anyone... I tried taking money out of one of my credit cards and in a matter of a few minutes, people crawled all over the place looking for us... I tried to contact Mark, but I couldn't get through to him... After a thorough analysis, we decided against trying to use our funds or to reach out to someone related to any of us... Somebody is clearly looking for us... Anyway, Nick and I have no one in the world. We couldn't turn to Adam's brother, either."

Ryan stopped, put up his hand to indicate that he would like her to sit where she was, and went to the living-room to check the bar. Sure enough, he found a bottle of scotch and came back triumphantly with it. "We have something to drink. Let's find glasses," he said with a false cheer.

After he left the bottle on the table, he went to the cupboard to look for two glasses.

Kate knew he was just acting right then. He wanted to hide his insecurity and anger but he wasn't very good at that. She also understood he needed to release some of his pent-up fury.

Ryan brought the glasses at the table and poured generous portions of whiskey.

"I don't really drink," Kate said softly.

He only shrugged and, putting one of the glasses in front of her, he said, "Once won't kill you."

"I hadn't thought it would," she murmured and took the glass in her hand. "What are we drinking for?"

Ryan thought for a moment and replied, "Why not for new beginnings?

We've had a new beginning today, haven't we?" he asked winking at her.

"Why not?" Kate murmured again and sipped from her glass.

Ryan watched her drink and then swallowed a mouthful and hissed. "Strong stuff," he said and took the bottle in his hand to check the label again. "Good stuff," he repeated, and replaced the bottle down on the table. He took another mouthful from his glass.

Kate sipped daintily a couple of times and then, her patience at an end, she asked, "Will you continue with the story?"

"Story? Yeah, you could say story, I suppose. It doesn't seem real," Ryan agreed after considering her words for a few seconds.

"I didn't mean it like that..." Kate started to say but he interrupted her with a gesture.

"I didn't say that, baby. I was simply making fun of myself... You know, after over a decade of covert operations, with a ratio of over eighty-five percent success, I found myself here, in a place resembling paradise but which turned out to be a living hell for all of us... We needed help for Adam, medical help. Good medical help, and the kind that doesn't talk but does a good job... Well, that kind of help is expensive. Of course, most of the cash Nick and I came with was gone in less than a week... We had to find a place to lay low, and after the experience with the credit card advance, we had to find another place... Of course, we didn't dare to withdraw money from any of our cards afterwards. Luckily, I still had an untraceable card with me... It held only a few thousand dollars and we knew the money wouldn't last...," Ryan explained with wide gestures and paused.

He drank some more whiskey to gain courage. He knew the hard part was just coming about.

"That's the card I used to open the account on the dating site, by the way," he said glancing at her for a second. "Initially, we thought of renting a yacht with that money, but I was positive they would keep an eye on men leasing yachts and we couldn't pick up a woman and ask her do that for us... Not in a very short period of time. We needed someone to trust and trust needs time to build...," he said and shrugged.

Kate wanted to touch and comfort him. Ryan seemed very deep in his memories, though, and she didn't move. She waited for him to continue.

After another sip of his drink, Ryan continued, "Anyway, we knew we had to find a solution... We needed a solution that didn't involve reaching out to someone who could be traced to us... So, at first, as a joke, just to have a bit of laugh on my expense, the guys mentioned I was thinking of finding the woman I wanted on the Internet and asked why I shouldn't do just that... After I'd found one I liked, I should try to ask her for help, they said... I would have killed two birds with one stone... I'd get the money to get out of here, money we'd return afterwards, of course, because we're not leeches, and I'd also get the girl."

Ryan stood up and went to turn the light on. Kate had been so drawn into his story that she hadn't realized the room was dark. The light of the day was slowly waning.

She blinked a few times and Ryan burst into laughter, "You look like a little owl blinking like that."

"Thank you very much for the comparison," Kate replied not too delighted to have been compared to an owl.

"I like owls, they're cute," Ryan shrugged and defended his choice of words. "You're cute too."

"You've already got the girl, Ryan, so you can turn down the charm," Kate said flatly.

"You think it was just charm, Kate? Do you really think I lied to you and tried to charm you so you'd do what I wanted?" Ryan replied back heatedly.

Kate didn't answer and he got upset.

"You know, if I had merely tried to charm a woman, it wouldn't have taken me so many months. I'd have done it sooner," he replied in a mean voice pointing to her.

"You're saying I'm easy?" she replied quarrelsome.

"No, Kate, I didn't say that. Quite the opposite. I'm saying if I'd only wanted to charm my way into a woman's heart to get the money, I'd have chosen an easy one. I wouldn't have needed four months to gather my courage to ask for the fucking money!" Ryan bellowed, even though he'd begun his tirade in a very calm voice.

He got closer to her and, looking straight into her eyes, asked, "Do you know how difficult these months were, Kate? There were times at the beginning when we didn't even know whether Adam would live or die. We had to make rations so we'd have food for more time. I was literally going crazy not knowing if the mission had just gone wrong or it was a trap for all of us. I strongly believe, though, it was a trap for all of us. Adam said he thought he'd been targeted from the beginning and his cover hadn't lasted twelve hours... You know, Kate, if you hadn't mattered to me, I'd have moved on, found someone else I could have convinced to give me the money sooner. It wasn't only for me, it was for them as well, and I've always been these men's leader, and I have a duty to them, you understand? It wasn't like we intended not to pay you back."

She nodded but kept silent.

"I chose to wait, to know you better, to let you know me... Well, as much as I could let you know... I felt drawn to you from the first moment I saw that picture you put on that site... I thought a woman who had the courage to put such a picture on a dating site was a very smart woman. I analyzed it carefully. I saw it was a passport photo. I was sure you'd be a beauty. What I wanted though wasn't only beauty but also brains. I've always wanted a woman I could talk to not a doll looking good on my arm. Candy arms I can find very easy. I've never had problems with that... So, I stuck with you and even if the guys pushed me either to open the conversation about the money with you or to find someone else, I didn't give up."

"That's... interesting, I'd say." Kate replied hesitantly. Ryan narrowed his eyes and prompted her to say in a rush, "What now?"

"No one followed you here, I made sure of that. Yet, I'm afraid to leave you alone. If anyone has made the connection between the money you brought here and the reason you came, you're in danger and I'll have to keep an eye on you. The problem is I'll have to stick with the guys as well."

"Interesting conundrum, then," Kate replied.

"Not really," Ryan said and shook his head. "I can't take you to our nest. That isn't for you, clearly. We only have a dirty little room. But I can bring the guys here, if you don't mind. We'd lay low for a few days to see if anyone is onto you, and if not, you can rent a small yacht without a crew... I don't know, act like an eccentric woman with a lot of knowledge in boating... We could get out of Malaysia in a few days, and reach Singapore. It's only 197 nautical miles in between. I have a guy there... No one knows about him, I'm damn sure about that... I know he could get papers for the guys and me to fly to Montreal for instance. So, what do you think?"

"Let's say I agree with all that, although for instance I could rent the yacht and you three could sail to Singapore without me," Kate replied.

"If that's what you want, fine with me. It's your choice. But, before I leave, I'll have to make sure first you're already on a plane to Montreal. I wouldn't agree to leave you here, no matter what. Even if I had to drag you to the airport kicking and screaming, I'll do it," Ryan replied sternly.

"Yeah, that would look good, for sure," Kate replied drily. "You'd be arrested before you'd set foot into the airport, Ryan." She noticed he wanted to interject, and she put up her hand to stop him. "All right, we'll see. For the moment, yes, I agree with you. You should bring your guys here. There are two bedrooms, I understand, plus the sofa in the living room. I could take the sofa...," Kate started to arrange things but Ryan cut her arrangements short.

"I don't think we'd both fit on that sofa, Kate, and after this afternoon, I hope you don't think I'd let you sleep away from me, sweetie, do you?" Ryan inquired and stared her down with his intense eyes.

Kate blushed but didn't answer. Ryan grinned at her with satisfaction and continued, "Adam should take the other bedroom and Nick will be just fine on the sofa. He's slept on worse than that. You'll be sleeping in my arms, in the bedroom we shared this afternoon, all right?"

She nodded but kept silent.

"I like this streak of yours, Kate. For a businesswoman, you have quite an old-fashioned streak, and I do love it. Don't you ever change, baby," he leaned and whispered close to her ear.

He brushed his fingers on her cheek and pushed a rebellious lock of hair behind her ear.

Then, he tilted his head over her and kissed her, softly at the beginning and then more forcefully. He parted her lips and sank his teeth into her lower one. He stroked her mouth with his tongue at leisure and made love to her mouth for a few moments. It seemed like an eternity to her.

After he was satisfied, Ryan drew back and whispered again, "I'd enjoy having you in my bed all the time, to do whatever I want, when I want."

"What?" she cried out. Her eyes were wide and reflected her shock. "Define that *'whatever you want'*, Ryan."

The man merely laughed and patted her cheek tenderly, "Don't worry, Kate, I'm not into kinky stuff," he said and then paused. That made her eyebrows shut up. "All right, not very kinky stuff, maybe just a little kinky stuff…" She stared at him speechless. He needed to reassure her some more, "I'll never do something you wouldn't want, baby, and that's a promise."

Kate didn't say a thing. She still stared at him. Ryan reached out and nudged her head to nod and said, "I hear you, Ryan, and I'm not worried."

His childish behavior reassured Kate and she laughed, "All right, all right, I hear you."

He pulled her up and fastened his hands behind her, "What are you saying about going back to bed, baby?"

Kate looked at him and touched his lips with her fingers, then with her mouth. She drew back and asked him, "But shouldn't you take care of your friends first?"

"Damn, I've already forgot about them. I can't even wrap my head around being so …. Yes, you're right, I must call the guys and ask them to move here," Ryan said and took his phone out of his pocket to make the call.

# CHAPTER THIRTEEN

"We'll stop here," Ryan turned to Kate after he stopped the car. "Nick will bring Adam out here, Kate. That means I'll leave you with them for a few minutes, so I could go and pick up the rest of our stuff. When I rented this room, I told them I was a painter and I don't want to raise any suspicions by leaving any kind of stuff inside that room. No self-respected artist would do such a thing," Ryan explained to her.

"But wouldn't your leaving in the dead of the night raise suspicions?" Kate asked him.

Ryan shrugged and explained, "I paid in cash and in advance for a month. I still have two more weeks paid. They'll assume I moved to another location. I already told the guy who rented the room to me that I didn't know how long I'd stay but I wanted the room available to me for another month. No, he won't get any ideas, Kate. He got his money and he didn't seem interested in more than that. Of course, he's never seen the guys and I always took care to park my car somewhere else. This type of car would have raised suspicions," Ryan replied and when he saw she wanted to ask something else, he put up his hand to stop her.

Kate noticed he glanced at the rear-view mirror and saw something. She swallowed her question.

"Stay here," Ryan said and got out of the car.

Kate looked after him. He walked in the direction of two men, coming slowly down the street. When he reached them, they exchanged a few words and he shouldered the man who appeared unsteady on his feet. Ryan with the help of the other man brought their wounded friend to the car.

"Kate, this is Adam and this is Nick," he introduced them to Kate when he reached the car. "Guys, this is Kate."

Kate waved and smiled at them. Both men were tall, almost as tall as Ryan, and both were sturdy. Adam, the hurt one, was almost as dark as Ryan, but Nick was dark blond. All three shared the same steely shine in their eyes. They were cut from the same cloth.

Adam was hurt and very pale, but Nick was the one who drew her eyes. The man was built like a bear. A long scar ran on his left cheek and would have made anyone step back in a confrontation with him.

"So, you're the sweet Kate," Adam said with a noticeable Southern accent and his eyes twinkled despite his pain, which had painted lines on his face.

"You're lucky you're hurt or I'd flatten you," Ryan growled at him. "Get into the car and stop making nice with my girl," he ordered curtly.

Kate thought Ryan was joking but the frown on his face belied her assumption. The truth dawned on her. Ryan was a jealous man. Kate questioned her wisdom about building a relationship with him. Jealous types were dangerous and she'd learned to avoid them.

Ryan helped Adam get into the car, ignoring Adam's grunts. He knew Adam would be embarrassed if people noticed his weakness.

"Nick will stay right here, next to the driver's side until I come back," Ryan said to Kate in an authoritative voice that didn't brooch any comment. "I want you protected at all times and if anything happens, Nick will drive you away."

"Ryan…," Kate started to say but Ryan interrupted her impatiently.

"I know, sweetie, but believe me, it's for the best, all right? Anyway, I'll be back soon and let's hope that everything goes smoothly."

With those parting words, Ryan turned around and vanished into the darkness. She looked after him with scared eyes.

"He'll be back," Nick told her in a gruff voice. He'd noticed she was worried and wanted to make her feel at ease. "He always comes back," he added.

"How do you know?" Kate asked him. His detached assessment hadn't appeased her worries.

Nick merely shrugged and then said, "I just know."

Kate didn't say anything. She decided to seize her chance to learn the truth and she focused first on Adam, determined to read his thoughts. It wasn't too difficult. She didn't feel he resisted like Ryan. She cheered happily in her mind and focused on unlocking Adam's secrets.

She was about to cheer herself again when she realized Ryan had told her the truth, but Adam put a hand to his forehead and grunted.

Kate got scared. Adam felt her intrusion and that wasn't good at all. The man looked up at her and frowned. She tried her best smile but, apparently, her best smile didn't work.

"What the hell is going on?" Adam snapped at her and his outburst attracted Nick's attention.

"What, Adam? What happened?" he asked.

"Something's damn wrong here, bro, believe me. I felt something like tentacles in my mind. Now, I have a terrible headache. She was staring at me at the time so...," Adam said, and left Nick to fill in the blanks.

Both men turned accusingly to her. Their terrible scowls made her cringe.

Kate never thought something like that would happen to her. First, she couldn't read Ryan's thoughts, and now that. She hadn't expected any problems with Adam.

"She's been doing something to me, Nick," Adam bellowed. "I don't know what but she has," he pointed an accusing finger to Kate.

Nick leaned over her and Kate retreated to the car door. His stance frightened her and her heart beat faster.

"What's going on here?" Ryan's voice penetrated her fear and brought a glimmer of hope. "Nick, why the hell are you threatening Kate?" Ryan barked. His expression didn't promise anything good to his mates.

"She's been doing something to me, Ryan," Adam repeated stubbornly. "I know she has. I haven't lost my mind yet. I saw her staring at me and then I felt something pushing into my head and now I have a headache, man," Adam explained upset and confused at the same time. He rubbed his temples to soothe the pain.

Ryan frowned and turned to Kate. He stared at her insistently and waited for her to say something in her defense. Adam's words seemed a bit out there, but Ryan didn't know Adam to be fanciful.

"I haven't done anything, Ryan," Kate said but noticed no one believed her. "I mean I haven't tried to hurt him or anything," she continued and their scowls turned uglier. Things didn't look good for her.

"Then what happened, Kate?" Ryan insisted. "Why is Adam having a headache and why does he feel you're responsible?"

"I don't know," Kate said and waved her hand. "I really don't know, Ryan," she repeated more forcefully when Ryan glared. She thought better and decided to tell him the truth. "Okay, Ryan, I'll tell you something but you'll think I'm a freak," Kate said wretchedly and then, fell silent for a few seconds.

"I'm waiting, Kate. Talk, now," he barked and his voice made her wince. The man was indeed a born leader.

Kate gathered her courage and said softly, barely audible at all, "I can read minds. I couldn't read yours, Ryan, which was a first, but I could read Adam's. Still, no one felt my probing before and no one had a headache afterwards, I promise."

The three men watched her in silence. Her revelation stunned them. They didn't reply and Kate felt dejected.

Then, Nick grumbled, "Well, anything's possible, guys. Do you remember that guy who worked for CIA? The one we had to free from that compound in South America? With those ugly glasses?"

Adam nodded and agreed with him, "Yeah, everything's possible."

Ryan remained skeptical for a few more moments. Then, he remembered that not far before he'd felt like someone was probing into his mind and frowned. "And you say you couldn't read my mind?" he asked Kate.

Kate shook her head. She admitted she'd tried several times, while they were talking over the phone and even when they met face to face but she hadn't been successful.

"You want to say that you can read someone's mind over the phone?" Adam looked at her with doubting eyes.

He believed there were people with certain abilities but he thought there was a limit to what they could do. Reading someone's mind over the phone didn't seem possible.

"Normally, yes," she replied and shrugged as if it had been a common occurrence. "For instance, one of the guys from the dating site was actually a serial killer and I could read his thoughts and delivered him to the police.

Anonymously, of course. I don't need that hassle," she explained.

"That's interesting," Nick said pensively. "You know what guys? When we get to Singapore, we should call Mark. She can listen into the call to see what she can read, huh?" he told his friends, his regularly somber face lit with a special light.

Ryan nodded absently. He was still looking intently at Kate. "So, you can't read my mind." he repeated.

"God, man, you have an obsession," Adam remarked disgustedly. "We're talking about serious things here, Ryan. Can you wrap your mind onto something else but your love affair?" he asked sardonically.

"This is bloody serious for me, Adam, so stay out of it," Ryan bit out and turned to her again, "Kate!"

"No, Ryan, I can't read your mind," she finally replied exasperated. "I wouldn't have reacted the way I did when you asked me for the money if I could," she continued with biting irony.

Ryan contemplated her for a few more seconds and nodded satisfied with her answer. Kate made a good point and he was content she wasn't able to read his mind. One question remained though. He didn't understand why she couldn't read his mind but could read Adam's, so he asked her.

Kate shrugged and replied, "I don't know why, Ryan. It's the first time something like that has happened to me. Such abilities don't come with a manual, you know," she ended in a sardonic voice to cover the truth.

She thought she'd found an explanation. Her inability to read him was due to her emotional connection to him. Yet, she didn't want to tell him that.

"All right, then," he accepted. He knew that he couldn't get an answer if there wasn't any. "Pile up, Nick, and let's go," Ryan said and went to the back of the car. He threw everything he was carrying in the trunk and returned.

He hesitated for a moment, his hand on the ignition key, and then, he turned to Kate and asked again, "You really can't read my mind?"

"No, I told you, I can't!" she replied exasperated.

She threw her arms in the air and rolled her eyes. Her patience was wearing thin and she didn't understand why he persisted to ask the same question over and over again.

"That's good, baby, really good," Ryan said, a wide smile on his lips. He leaned over and kissed her lips.

His behavior prompted Adam to snicker and Nick to scowl, yet Ryan didn't care about what any of them thought or did. He started the car and drove back to Kate's house on the beach.

***

"Wow," Adam said when he saw the house and especially, the back of the house. "This is really cool, man! We have a pool and the sea is close. Look at here, the beach is private," he noticed enthusiastically and turned to Kate. He winked at her and said, "You know how to live in style, Kate."

Kate shook her head but beamed at him and replied, laughing, "Not really, Adam. You see, I haven't had a vacation for a long time, so I thought: why not? If I decided to go to Malaysia, why wouldn't I take a memorable vacation? That's why the house is the way it is," she explained.

"Good for you," Adam approved and gave her the high five. Rubbing his hands, he said, "And good for us. Guys, do you mind if I remain here on the deck for a while? I've been cooped up in that stinky little room for a few weeks and I'd really enjoy some fresh air."

"Not a problem, Adam," Ryan replied. "Take your time. I must go and buy some food from somewhere because what we had back there is not enough. All of Kate's reserves are depleted," he explained to his friends and picked up his car keys to leave.

Nick looked at Kate dumbfounded. He shook his head, and then turned after Ryan and asked, "Really? How much could she eat?"

Ryan burst into laughter at the scowl on Kate's lips and replied to Nick, "She didn't have too much to begin with, Nick, and I helped, of course."

"Ah, that explains it," Adam concluded with a grin of his, and lounged on a chaise-long, crossed his arms on his chest and breathed deeply. "God, how I missed this. This is just paradise, guys."

He closed his eyes and settled down, intent on listening to the murmur of the waves and breathing in the salty smell of the sea. In a few moments, Adam dozed off.

Kate, Nick and Ryan looked at him for a few seconds, then, Ryan took Kate's hand in his and pulled her inside the house. Nick followed them but began to feel like the proverbial third wheel when Ryan brushed his lips over Kate's hand.

"Anything to drink here?" Nick asked, looking around to cover his insecurity and embarrassment.

Kate jumped at his voice. She'd forgotten about Nick's presence and Ryan smiled with satisfaction. He knew he was the cause for her being so absent-minded.

"There's some whiskey there, Nick. Kate will show you, won't you Kate?" he turned to her and winked. "It's the good stuff, Nick. Powerful stuff, though, so take care. Anyway, I'll buy some beer if I find some," Ryan said.

"Maybe you can find some soft drinks as well?" Kate asked him. "I'm really not too fond of whiskey or beer," she explained.

"I'll see what I can do," Ryan replied on his way to the door and left, leaving them alone.

Kate remained standing, looking after him pensively. Nick interrupted her thoughts, "So, where's that whiskey, Kate? Adam could use a glass as well…," he said and then added, "If he wakes up, that is."

Kate turned to the kitchen and threw over her shoulder, "Follow me, big guy. I'll prepare the drinks for both of you."

Nick frowned behind her. He didn't understand her but then, he hadn't had too much to do with that type of woman. He'd avoided the wholesome women all his life. He'd considered they didn't worth the trouble, as he hadn't planned to get married and go the whole nine yards. He was satisfied with some fun now and then. His affairs didn't have a long-life span.

He shook his head and followed Kate into the kitchen. She took two glasses out of the cupboard.

"The bottle is there," Kate showed him. "Here's the glasses, Nick. I suppose you'd better pour yourself. You know how much you want to drink, I think. Anyway, better than I do."

Nick took the glasses from her and poured a drink for Adam and a taller one for him. He was about to leave when he turned and told her over the shoulder, "Thanks, Kate. And don't you dare read my mind," he stared her down.

Kate blushed violently at his parting words. She was trying to do just that and his words made her feel guilty.

Nick stared at her with narrowed eyes and left. Kate decided against going out to join the two men on the deck. Instead, she went to the bedroom, took a shower and went to bed.

\*\*\*

She'd already fallen asleep when Ryan's strong arms stole around her. Her head fell on his chest. It felt good. She felt protected. Contentedly, she sighed and went back to sleep.

# CHAPTER FOURTEEN

"It's been three days already, guys," Adam told them with a frown. "Look, I'm much better. No one's come after us so far, so we're good. I think it's time to go," he continued. "I want to get out of this God forsaken country and the sooner, the better. I've had enough."

He was sick of lying around all the time without anything to do. He needed a change but, most of all, he needed to be on the other side of the ocean. He wanted to go home.

Nick glanced at Ryan to see what he thought about Adam's sudden outburst because he, for one, was worried. He understood Adam's brush with death and the following several weeks, during which Adam had been bedridden, had had a serious impact on their friend.

To Nick's dismay, Ryan didn't show any signs he was aware of what was going on with Adam. He seemed busy watching Kate swimming in the pool. She was skimpily-clad in a blue swimming suit and Ryan's eyes couldn't leave her alone.

When Nick noticed Ryan's chief concern, he rolled his eyes annoyed. He growled, "Come on, man! Snap out of it for now. You've had her for four days already. Not even you can be so smitten," he remarked with disdain.

"What the fucking hell are you talking about?" Ryan turned to Nick furiously, his eyes narrowed to slits. "She's not the entertainment here, Nick," he barked at his friend.

Nick took a step back and put his hands up to show Ryan he didn't mean anything demeaning about Kate.

"Don't you get it?" Ryan continued. "She's the one for me, and you have to respect that, got it?" he punctuated his affirmation by nudging Nick in his chest with his finger.

"How hard the mighty fall," Adam remarked sotto voce and shook his head.

Yet, his words reached Ryan's ears and he turned to him irately, "I don't care what any of you two bulkheads think about me, Adam. It's my business not yours," he concluded and glanced at Kate again. "Anyway, I can't wait to see what you'll do once you found a woman who means the world to you! What you'd do then…"

"That's not me," Adam interrupted him, and shook his head for good measure. "Forget it, Ryan. I'll never lose my mind over any chick. Period. It's not worth it."

Nick nodded in complete agreement.

"She's not a chick, dumbass. That's what neither of you can get through your thick skulls," Ryan replied. He stood up and flexed his fists and that prompted Adam to frown at his fighting stance.

"Oh, oh, oh, guys," Nick tried to calm them down. "No harm done, Ryan. It was just stupid talking, man," he observed and stood up. Nick went to Ryan and put a hand on his shoulder in a friendly manner. "Come on, Ryan, don't forget Adam is still not one hundred percent and it wouldn't be fair…"

"Let him come," Adam snapped and stood up, although his movements were not as fluid as his friends'. He panted in frustration. "I can take him," he specified and copied Ryan's stance.

"Really?" Ryan replied and shoved Adam. That made him fall back in his seat like a puppet. "You can take me, huh," he said derisively. "See? I can wrestle you even with one arm tied behind my back. You've got no chance, man, wake up," he told Adam.

"Guys, guys, guys, this is not the time to do that. Just chill out," Nick intervened, taking a position between them.

"What's going on?" Kate inquired alarmed and all three turned to her guiltily.

They were shocked to see her there. They'd been so caught in their squabble that they hadn't heard her come out of the pool and step on the deck.

She waited for them to answer but no one volunteered an explanation. Adam and Nick looked anywhere else but her and not just out of remorse. They didn't want to further aggravate Ryan's possessiveness.

Their friend was beyond smitten and even though they'd noticed Kate looked good and was funny, they didn't share his attraction and couldn't understand his recent behavior.

"Ryan, I asked you what was going on," she repeated stubbornly and stared Ryan down.

Kate felt undercurrents and was afraid the men had had a fallen out. She would have tried to read Adam and Nick's minds but she didn't want to be exposed doing it once more.

"Nothing, Kate, don't worry," Ryan finally replied and waved his hand. "We were just fooling around... We didn't have anything better to do and we got restless, that's all," he explained to her.

Adam glanced at her first and then at Ryan, and shook his head. He gave up understanding what was going on between the two of them.

"Drop it, man," Nick warned him in a whisper and touched his shoulder "Let's talk about leaving, Ryan. I think it's time, even past time," he observed.

"Oh, that's what bothers you," Kate surmised and her face lit up. She was relieved there wasn't any other reason of contention between them.

No one tried to set her straight.

"I was wondering about leaving as well," Kate said. "I'm a bit antsy and I can't wait to see the second part of the plan unfold," she confessed and glanced from one man to the other.

"Well, I've done some research these day and come out with a company that rents good yachts at reasonable prices," Ryan started explaining and waved the others to sit down. "At about seven thousand, eight thousand tops, we could rent a forty-foot monohull with three cabins, two heads and all the necessary equipment. More important, I think, it's sturdy enough to take us to Singapore," Ryan continued. "Of course, the price is only for the yacht. We'll have to pay separately for fuel and food, and I understand they can provide that too... It would cost a little more, about nine hundred for the fuel at least," he said pensively. "I don't think it would be a good idea to let them know we'd stop in Singapore so we'll have to buy a little more fuel and food... The food will be about five hundred...," he specified and looked at them. He wanted to see what they thought about the costs.

Adam and Nick didn't move a muscle. They had that immobile façade they would show whenever they plotted a mission.

Ryan hadn't expected any kind of serious opposition from them and indeed, at his inquiring expression, they nodded slightly. Having their answer, Ryan turned to Kate to see what she had to say. She merely shrugged. Anyway, she didn't know anything about all that.

Having his answer, Ryan continued, "So we're looking at a total of nine thousand fifty tops," he concluded and again waited for their reactions.

"Okay, that works, I think," Kate replied pensively. "I can put the charge on my credit card, it won't be a problem. There's one thing I'll have to do though," she said. "I'll have to let my bank know beforehand, so they don't decline the payment. Once the bank is warned about the amount I need to pay, I don't see any issues coming from that quarter," Kate assured them.

"You'll get your money back, Kate, don't worry," Nick told her morosely. "We don't take money from people and run away," he assured her. He didn't seem comfortable with taking her money and his face darkened.

"I haven't even thought about that, Nick," Kate waived his concerns away. "I'm not worried about that, period. I was just saying I have to let the bank know so the payment would clear, nothing else."

"I understand that," Nick replied stubbornly. "I've only wanted to make sure you also understand you'll get the money back from us as soon as we're on the other side of the ocean."

"Oh, I'm tired of this money thing, honestly. Why does money always have to come first?" Kate snapped. "Could we talk about something more important, like how we'd plan this? I'm pretty sure it takes a little more than my booking the boat on the Internet," she pointed out.

Nick scowled at her but dropped the subject. He turned to Ryan and waited for his input as he was the strategist in the group and they always counted on his ideas.

"First, Kate must learn a few things about yachting," he explained and glanced at her. "You have to, Kate. You will go and sign the papers for the leasing. You will also have to check the yacht. The three of us have to avoid being seen as much as possible," Ryan said.

Adam and Nick nodded. They knew they shouldn't be seen. The plan could succeed only if no one was the wiser about their whereabouts. Kate nodded as well, although she wasn't very confident she could learn everything about yachting, even in theory only, in a very short time. Then, they waited for Ryan to continue.

"Kate, I think you should tell those people you want to surprise your boyfriend with a cruise for his birthday," he addressed Kate directly and took her hand in his. "Of course, you'll let them know you have basic training and understanding in sailing, but make sure to specify your boyfriend will be the one who's going to man the yacht... I think that would be helpful. They shouldn't get suspicious if, for instance, you can't answer some of their questions or you come through as being too green. No one of us can ask more from you, Kate," he said and glanced at his friends who approved his statement.

Kate nodded and looked at the other two guys as well. They put their thumbs up to let her know they were confident she could do her part.

Ryan continued, "As we need three cabins, it would be also a good idea if you let it slip you've invited two more couples to join you two for seven days of fun... I don't know," he shrugged, "Just chat like women usually do. Try to make them think you're worry free, and you're thinking only of having fun and being with friends for a few days...Does that work for you?" he asked her.

"Yes, why not? I'm a fast learner so I don't think I'd tip my hand too easy. They won't even guess I don't have any experience with yachting or whatever. I was on a boat before but I've never manned one, of course..." Kate pondered upon Ryan's words a few moments more, and then she said, biting her bottom lip, "No worries about the chatting up. I will imitate Ellie's style of speaking. That girl can't keep a secret if her life depended on that. Everybody knows what's going on in her life and what she's thinking," she explained.

"Ellie?" Adam asked.

"Ah, my best friend," Kate answered when she remembered they didn't know Ellie.

"Focus here, people," Ryan ordered and tapped the table top. "You can gossip later."

His words made both Kate and Adam scowl at him but he didn't care.

"Good. Then, let's go inside, Kate, so you can make the reservation online. At least, we could have that out of the way, and then we'll take it from there, all right?" he asked and glanced at each one of them to see if they agreed. Once he was satisfied they approved, he continued, "I've made the calculations and if we sail at five knots, not more, even if we stop twice for complete rest, it shouldn't take us more than let's say three days, to be generous with time... And, Kate, again, it is not a boat, it's a yacht. Don't you tell the guys from the renting office something like that."

Kate nodded although she didn't enjoy his correction. Boat, yacht, the same thing. Then, she went inside.

Ryan didn't follow immediately. He remained seated and enjoyed the sight of her backside for a few more moments.

"Snap out of it, man. It's already getting beyond embarrassing. We got it. You're crazy about her. But let's go! You'll have enough time for that later," Nick grumbled. "It isn't like you haven't seen it before or that this is the last time you'll ever see it," he pointed out.

Ryan glowered at him but didn't reply. He didn't want to fuel a new discussion. Besides, bruised in his male ego, he wondered if he did come through like being completely wiped out.

He followed Kate into the house. When he reached the bedroom, she was already in the shower and the water was running. After a few seconds, he took off his clothes with impatient gestures and opened the shower door.

"Mind if I join you?" he asked her politely. He intended to get in the shower with her anyway but thought he should ask at least.

Kate wiped the water off her face, looked up at him and smiled. "Why not? I'd love to," she replied and Ryan grinned at her.

He joined her in the shower stall and closed the door behind him. He pulled her to him forcefully. Kate had already learned he liked it that way, and she didn't dislike it either.

Ryan kissed her soundly, feasting on her mouth like a starved man. His hands roamed all over her back and his touch banked small fires under her skin.

***

"Okay, I think I got it. I can answer any questions they might have and I can make a thorough check of the boat," Kate concluded, when she shut down the computer late in the afternoon.

"Not a boat, but a yacht, baby, I've told you already. Men are sensitive about this shit. You know, boys and their toys…" Ryan said, looking up from his laptop and grinning at her.

"Well, whatever," Kate shrugged. "I know the basics and everything's fine. The reservation is made, the charge cleared just fine, so I can go get the boat… sorry, yacht," she corrected herself, "the day after tomorrow, early in the morning. Then we can finally leave Malaysia and turn towards greener pastures," she summarized the situation.

Adam grunted in satisfaction. Their predicament was about to end. He went and took a beer from the fridge to celebrate.

Ryan noticed he moved with much more ease than before. He was grateful his friend had pulled out because, for a moment there, the situation had been touch and go.

When Ryan saw Adam was hit, not by one bullet but three, he hadn't thought Adam would make it through, even with the best medical help their money could buy.

Neither Nick nor Ryan believed Adam would survive his wounds. Considering their living conditions during the last few weeks, they were convinced Adam would have died because of an infection, even if he hadn't died because of his wounds.

Luckily, Adam was a strong and stubborn bastard. Probably, those two basic features helped him stay alive.

"I think you should rest until we get to the yacht, Adam. You need to regain your strength and soon. Only God knows what we might encounter," Ryan bellowed after Adam.

Adam's head popped up from behind the door, "I've rested enough, mother. I need to move. I'm dying inside not doing anything all day," he replied patting his chest.

"You'll have enough time to do whatever you want after you've regained your health," Kate interfered and that gained her a scowl from Adam.

Kate didn't take exception at his scowl, but smiled sweetly at him. She'd already learned he was only bark and no bite, at least with her.

"Kate, no offense, you've been very helpful, and you're very sweet... No need to scowl at me, Ryan, it's not like I'd ever poach on another's man's territory, and you know it," he glanced at Ryan and reproached to him in a steely voice.

By then, Adam had learned how Ryan reacted when it came to Kate. He knew Ryan would have something to say and Adam wanted to smother any kind of squabble before it began.

"Anyway, Kate, sweetheart," he turned back to her "I know what I need better than you."

Ryan snarled at Adam's endearment for Kate, but didn't make any comment. His friends' remarks about him being totally spellbound with Kate nudged at him.

Yet, Kate sensed something and turned to him inquiringly. Instantly, Ryan's expression turned blank. He thought he'd better not open a new can of worms and decided to speak about his concerns with Adam when he had a chance to catch him alone. He wanted to settle that thing once and for all.

He knew Adam didn't have any nefarious intentions, yet Ryan didn't like to hear another man talking to Kate like that. She belonged to him and that was what mattered.

# CHAPTER FIFTEEN

Kate had already checked the yacht and signed the papers, and now she waited on the deck, drinking some Coca-Cola and admiring the marina. She was bored out of her mind.

She wondered when the guys would come. She didn't enjoy the solitude and that was something new. She used to like being alone now and then. In her line of work, solitude seemed a blessing sometimes.

She knew the men had to make sure no one waited for them, but she'd already been waiting for three hours and was fed up.

She'd already checked her emails and answered to a few of them. She'd checked her Facebook account and tried to entertain herself with a few amusing videos, but it didn't work. She was tense and worried about Ryan. The slow passing of time was unbearable.

The sun was almost above her head and she silently thanked the person who'd installed an umbrella on the deck.

At least she wouldn't get a heatstroke waiting there in the sun.

A sudden rocking movement under her feet prompted her to look up. Ryan finally came aboard with his duffel bag in hand.

He smiled at her when their eyes met. He came closer and touched her cheek tenderly. Then, he leaned over her and kissed her as if he hadn't seen her for days not only a few hours.

After he tasted her to his satisfaction, Ryan whispered to her, "Everything's fine, baby. Adam will follow in about five minutes and Nick will be the last to come aboard. Then, we'll sail away and figure out our future. What do you think?"

Kate nodded and took a moment to return the favor. She kissed him back and stroked his lips with her fingers. She let them linger on his lips for a few more seconds before pulling her hand back.

"Maybe you'd like to join me on the deck after you take your duffel bag downstairs. I chose the largest cabin for us. Oh, you'll find beer in that cooler over there," Kate told him and beamed at him when she saw the light in his eyes.

If the guys hadn't been supposed to come soon and they hadn't been scheduled to sail out in under an hour, Ryan would have taken their light flirtation further.

He always responded to her with passion and that pleased Kate. It wouldn't have been fun if her desire for him had been one-sided. After she'd enjoyed the fine conversationalist Ryan, as well as the hot-headed Ryan, now, she enjoyed the lover.

She wished to be with Ryan in the future. Kate knew they could build something together based on what they'd already shared.

She couldn't wait to put that sordid story way behind them and to start a new life, just the two of them.

She still speculated over their future when she heard heavy footsteps on the deck again. Kate looked up and Adam grinned at her. His hair looked thoroughly mussed.

He'd been stressed out and he'd run his fingers through his hair repeatedly. She discerned tense lines near the corners of his mouth. Kate smiled at him and waved an enthusiastic welcome.

"If you want, you can go below deck and leave your stuff," she pointed to the backpack Adam was carrying. "Then you should come back out here and have a beer," she continued, always smiling warmly at him.

"Will do, boss," he replied and saluted her with friendly mockery.

Her smile widened. Her welcome had already chased part of Adam's tension. He saluted her again and went below deck to leave his stuff.

Ryan's enthusiastic voice talking to Adam reached Kate's ears. She overheard them poking around, as men would do in such circumstances and she smiled amused. She'd never understood those male rituals, but she took them as they were.

Adam and Ryan were still talking and laughing below deck, when Nick climbed onto the deck. His bear-like appearance always startled her, although she'd noticed he was the most level-headed and kindest of the three. Ryan had a serious temper and Adam was fast in giving burning replies.

Nick came to her, tapped her cheek with his fingers and said, "Hello, little sun pie. You know, I think you should remain under the umbrella. Your face is already red like a lobster. Anyway, at least, the sun coloured your hair just fine. Now, you have streaks of red and many other nuances..."

"What the hell do you think you're doing?" Ryan's voice boomed behind him.

Nick turned around, completely unaffected, and stared Ryan down, "You know very well I'm not doing anything, bro. Just having a little chit-chat. Cool off!"

Before Ryan could answer, Nick took his backpack and went below deck, passing by Adam who was looking from him to Ryan and back.

"You know he didn't mean anything," Adam tried to appease Ryan's livid fury. "Nick isn't like that," he pointed out although he supposed Ryan should have known that by then.

"I know," Ryan snapped. "That's why I freaked out. Had it been you..."

"Yeah," Adam laughed merrily, "I'm the horny toad..."

"Ryan...," Kate started hesitantly. "What's the matter? I don't understand any of this."

She had no idea what was wrong. She knew she'd had a light conversation with Nick, and Ryan didn't like it. Ryan's reaction made her feel uncomfortable.

"You liked flirting with him, didn't you?" Ryan accused her with fire in his eyes.

"What?" she gasped and her eyes widen with shock.

"He flirted with you and you flirted back," Ryan accused her flatly.

"Are you mad?" Kate inquired with disbelief. "Nick didn't flirt with me. Why would he? He just noticed the sun burnt my skin. That's not flirting, Ryan. It's just casual conversation," she explained to him as if he'd had only half a brain.

"Damn! The woman doesn't even know when a man flirts with her," Ryan shook his head in desperation, and turned his back to her furiously, his hands braced on his hips and his head down.

"He didn't, Ryan," she replied hotly. "And if this is what you think of me, then..."

"Don't go there, Kate," he warned her turning back and pointing to her. "Don't even think about it."

"You're jealous," understanding suddenly loomed on her. "You're just jealous and making a scene," she advanced toward him, angry as a cat.

"And if I am?" he answered back gruffly and his tone made her stop, taken aback.

"I don't know," she threw her hands in the air giving up. "What the hell," she turned her back to him and took a few steps on the deck.

She didn't like that streak of jealousy in Ryan at all. Possessiveness of any kind was unpleasant and she considered it was dangerous in the long run.

She returned to him, and copying his posture, hands on hips and head held high, she said, "Well, actually, Ryan, I do know. I don't like your possessiveness. At all. I'm not an object. I have to have freedom to speak to other people without being afraid you'll drop them if your fancy strikes," she spelled her terms.

"Kate, it's not like that and you know it," Ryan tried to appease her. "Yes, I do consider that you belong to me…"

"I belong!" she yelled. "I belong, you say!"

The men cringed every time she raised her voice. They hadn't heard her shouting before, but she seemed to have good lungs.

Adam whispered to Ryan, "There are people around, bro. Quiet her down or our plan could end before it even started."

Ryan nodded to him imperceptibly and then went toward Kate, holding his hands up conciliatorily. "Baby, you misunderstand. Just listen," he rushed to say when he saw her shaking her head. "Yes, I said that you belonged to me, but that means I belong to you too. We belong together and to each other. That's what I meant. You don't have to go nuts because I didn't say it better. I'm a man, Kate. I don't know any fancy talk. I sometimes speak without really thinking, you know," he explained apologetically and stroked her shoulder to calm her down.

Kate narrowed her eyes at him with suspicion. She sensed he had some agenda but then, she cooled down and said, "All right, Ryan. Let's say I believe you. It's not like I can read your damn mind," she ended the argument angrily and stomped below deck to spend a few moments alone.

Back on the deck, Ryan grinned with satisfaction. He was mostly satisfied because she couldn't read his mind.

The other two men exhaled relieved. The argument had ended and now they could finally sail away.

"Let's have a beer first," Nick proposed, "and then let's get out of here. I can't wait to get to Singapore and be on a plane to the States."

"Canada." Ryan corrected him.

"What the...?" Adam who was leaning over the cooler to grab a beer interjected, but Ryan's gesture stopped him.

"Listen up! Canada's the best choice for two reasons. First, I have to know Kate is back in Montreal where she's safe. Second, I think Canada's a better place to arrange a meeting with Mark, guys. Neutral territory," Ryan explained glancing from one to the other.

Adam started to shake his head in disagreement but then, he thought better and stopped. After another moment, he came to him and tapped him hard on the shoulder, "You're a genius, man! A freaking genius!"

Ryan scowled at him and wanted to give him an acid reply but reconsidered. He didn't care what Adam was saying if he had his cooperation. He turned to Nick and looked at him inquiringly.

"I'm in," Nick nodded and replied in his usual grave voice. "It's a sound plan. Anyway, we do have to keep the girl safe. That comes first. She risked enough coming here blindly, you know. And no, Ryan," he said putting up his hand, "I'm not saying that because I have the hots for her, man," Nick shook his head. "She's your girlfriend and that's all I need to know."

Ryan nodded. He understood where he stood with Nick. Then, he asked Adam to give him a beer from the cooler.

# CHAPTER SIXTEEN

"Okay, in an hour tops, we'll dock in Singapore," Nick told Ryan watching the horizon and opening a bottle of beer. "It's good we get there in the evening. We're less likely to be noticed. What do you think?" he asked.

"Yes, I think it's a good timing," Ryan consented. "Adam is much better now and I saw he started exercising yesterday afternoon. I'm just a bit concerned he might exaggerate and reopen one of the wounds, though," Ryan said pensively and bit into a juicy mango.

"I wouldn't worry about him, Ryan," Nick shook his head. "He's fine. He's aware of what he can do or not. He was very careful. I watched him."

"If you say so." Ryan replied but didn't seem convinced.

"Is Kate all right?" Nick asked him. "I haven't seen her since early this morning. It's been a few hours already. She didn't seem to be sea sick but…"

"She's alright, just a bit tired," Ryan waved his concern away and finished off the mango throwing the core into the sea under Nick's disapproving eyes.

Nick had a very special concern for the environment and didn't take lightly anything related to littering even if it was something biodegradable. Yet, he kept his tongue. He knew he'd risk a lengthy tirade from Ryan who didn't share his strict views.

"Tired?" Nick chose to ask. "How come?" he expressed his confusion. "We haven't let her do anything on the deck for the entire trip, man. She only spent some time reading under that umbrella and she swam for about an hour yesterday afternoon when we stopped…"

"Well, there's tired and there's tired," Ryan mused, unwilling to go into too many details. There were matters he didn't like to discuss even with his best friends.

"Ah, that tired," Nick concluded when the truth dawned on him. "You seem a bit insatiable, if I may say so. We heard you with all the insulation on the yacht," he shook his head in concern.

"Why do you care?" Ryan turned towards him with narrowed eyes.

"I don't, why would I? I was just saying. I haven't known you to be like that. You're the type to love them fast and leave them. I don't remember you've ever gone back for seconds," Nick observed, watching Ryan with his impenetrable eyes.

"Well, they weren't Kate, were they?" Ryan barked back.

"Oh, man, don't start with me. I was just wondering what's changed, that's all," Nick replied in a conciliatory voice.

"What don't you understand? It's not quantum physics, after all. She's it," Ryan bit out, exasperated he had to spell everything out. He thought Nick the smartest between his two friends but now he wondered if he should reconsider that assessment.

"It seems so," Nick murmured and went to adjust a sail only to get away from him.

Ryan muttered furiously to himself. He was an easy target for his friends. He lost his temper whenever Kate became the topic of conversation with any of them.

They probably started those discussions because he'd built a certain reputation with women in the past. They couldn't understand the change in him. Ryan also knew he perceived everything as a reproach or had the feeling he was the butt of their jokes.

He knew he needed to stop being so belligerent. He feared his jealous behavior might drive Kate away and that was the last thing he wanted.

"Why are you grumbling, baby?" Kate's voice came from behind him. She wrapped her arms around his shoulders and kissed his cheek.

He turned to her and looked at her seriously, pondering what he should say and decided to go with the truth. "I was just muttering to myself, because I keep making an ass of myself. I'm afraid you'll walk away," he confessed involuntarily and felt like slapping himself over his head. He wanted to be honest with her but even honesty had limits.

"I see," Kate said and, leaning on him, she hugged him tightly. "I won't walk away, Ryan. I know you're mostly bluster," she replied cheerfully.

"What??!" the man shouted incredulously.

She looked up at him and laughed, "Like right now. You shout and grumble and scowl… but, in the end, that's all there is to it and I don't see why I'd walk away. It's not like I'm in any sort of danger when I'm with you, right?" she asked.

"Right," Ryan agreed and turning around, he hugged her, holding her tight to his chest.

"Ouch! That hurts, Ryan. I still want to have intact ribs when I go and grab a cola from the cooler, baby," Kate joked, and her frivolous reply made Ryan lighten up and laugh as well.

He finally let her go and said, "In less than an hour we'll be in Singapore, Kate. You'll have to call the guys with the yacht to return it and then, we need to get on a plane to Montreal."

"There's no direct flight to Montreal, Ryan," she said smartly.

"I know that, smart ass!" he bit back. "I meant we'd take a plane that would help us get to a connection for Montreal later," he explained through gritted teeth.

"I know, Ryan, but I like to make you explode. That's fun. You're such a pretty picture fuming like this." Kate said laughing.

"I told you my blood pressure had never been the same since I met you, didn't I?"

"Yeah, you did," Kate nodded. "But what's a bit of blood pressure between us when we can have so much fun together, hmmm?" she mused coyly.

"Right," he said dryly. "It's only my blood pressure, not yours. It seems you react better than I do... to everything."

She shrugged and smiled mischievously at him. Then, she turned away throwing over her shoulder, "It happens, baby, what can I say?"

He swatted her backside and she jumped up.

"Hey, what are you doing?" she scowled at him.

"Just fooling around, Kate. Come on!"

The woman rubbed the spot he spanked and said, "Next time, fool around by putting less sting into your swat, Ryan, or I might retaliate in kind."

"Like how?" Ryan inquired lifting an eyebrow.

"Well, I can spank you as well," she replied in a dry voice.

"Kate, Kate, Kate," Adam's voice came from behind her. "I didn't know you had such a kinky side, girl," he laughed heartily.

Kate glanced at him and blushed so violently that even the tips of her ears turned red. She tried to salvage the situation, "We were just joking around, Adam."

"Come on, girl. There's no shame in spicing the game a little. Didn't Ryan teach you that?" Adam asked and winked at her.

Seeing she was mortified, Ryan interceded, "Drop it, Adam. Stop embarrassing her."

Kate shook her head and turned to go back below deck, but Ryan took her hand and turned her to him, "Kate, Adam's just joking. And even so, what we do, the two of us, it's our business and you don't have to feel ashamed of anything, you hear me?" he demanded in a very serious voice.

She nodded but still went downstairs to her cabin. She didn't think she could face Adam just then.

"Did you have to make her leave?" Ryan scowled at Adam.

"That wasn't my intention," Adam shook his head. "I didn't know she was so sensitive. I'll be more careful from now on, Ryan. She seems a little old-fashioned, if you ask me."

"I know she is, and that's her charm, you stupid," Ryan replied in a stern voice.

"What's the problem now?" Nick asked from behind Ryan. His voice had a hint of exasperation. "With you two, there's always something. It's like a fucking drama all the time around here," he observed and his tone implied that he didn't like it. He was sick of all their petty squabbles. He longed for the times when something like that didn't happen.

Ryan pushed him away and went after Kate, leaving them on the deck to do whatever they wanted.

# CHAPTER SEVENTEEN

"We're approaching Singapore, Ryan. Come out on the deck. We need another pair of hands here," Nick's voice thundered from above deck and made Kate grimace.

"Does he always have to thunder like that? Can't he talk in a normal tone of voice?" she asked Ryan.

Ryan just shrugged and went above deck to help his mates with the approach and anchorage. After about a quarter of an hour, he bellowed down to her, "We're here, Kate. Call the guys to return the yacht and let's move! Now!"

Her voice came as loud as his, "Who made you general, Ryan? Would it be difficult for you to phrase your requests differently? Would it kill you?" she ended her speech with a screech to be sure he heard her.

"My god, the lungs she has on her," Adam exclaimed completely stunned with the volume of her reply. "Anyway, we'll have to get our stuff from under the deck as well, so let's move, general," he said to Ryan and saluted him mockingly.

Ryan frowned at him but then burst into laughter, "She's something else, isn't she?"

"That she is," Nick grumbled and went below deck to take his bag. "We really need to move, guys. We don't know if they found out we'd come this way or ...."

"I know," Ryan said quickly to stop Nick from developing an entire lecture. He followed him downstairs to help Kate with their things.

\*\*\*

"I called the company and a guy will be here in five minutes. It seems they have an office in the marina so everything will be dealt with soon."

"That's good, Kate. The sooner we leave this city, the safer we'll be, you know," Ryan replied and started stuffing things into his duffel bag.

Kate looked incredulously at him for a few moments and then asked in a haughty voice, "Don't you think you should fold those shirts? Before stuffing them in there like there's no tomorrow?"

"No, I don't," he replied flittingly. "Anyway, I'll be travelling for at least the next twenty-four hours and I'll look dishevelled anyway. So, what's the point to trouble myself with packing carefully?" he asked.

Kate shrugged and said, "As you wish. At least I managed to fold these before you came. Put them on top so you have something clean and only slightly wrinkled to put on."

"I like it when you're behaving like a little wife," Ryan said looking at her and grinned.

"Little wife, Ryan? Really?" she snapped and braced her hands on her hips.

"Come on, baby, it wasn't meant like an insult," Ryan tried to explain. "Quite the opposite. It was just my way of saying I'd like it to be true."

Kate froze and the dress she had just folded fell on the floor unnoticed. She couldn't say or do anything but stare at him.

He cringed and murmured, "No romance in that, I know. Fucking hell! I'm so stupid," he slapped himself over the head.

Coming out of her shock, Kate knelt next to him, took his hand and said softly, "You don't have to try for something romantic, Ryan. I prefer the real you and what you've just said was... Well, it was very sweet. I just hadn't expected it, that's all."

"So, had I been smarter and said it as I should have, would you have said *yes*?"

Kate looked at him intently searching his face to read the truth behind his words. That was another moment when she regretted she couldn't read his mind. Yet, satisfied with what she saw on his face, she nodded, "When you find it in yourself to ask, yes, I will say *yes*. And you don't have to set a scene or anything, Ryan. You just have to be you."

"Does that mean I can ask you anytime? Even right now?" he asked with hope in his voice.

She nodded but kept silent and just watched him intently.

Ryan took her hand, kissed every one of her fingers, and then looked up at her and asked, "Will you marry me as soon as possible, Kate? Spend your life with me, play havoc with my blood pressure and bring me back to earth whenever I go around the bend?"

Her eyes glimmered with unshed tears and she nodded. She didn't know whether her voice would work.

"And will you have kids with me? I'm getting old, baby, and I'd love to be able to enjoy their young years while I don't need a cane or a wheelchair to chase after them."

Kate laughed, nodded again, leaned forward and gently brushed her lips to his, only once. Then she simply kept the connection between their mouths, to feel him close.

They were both so focused one on the other that they didn't even notice Adam and Nick in the doorway. Both men's faces betrayed their shock. They shook their heads in befuddlement. Adam elbowed Nick and signaled him to come out onto the deck and leave them alone.

# CHAPTER EIGHTEEN

"Well, that went well," Adam observed as soon as they'd reached the airport and managed to buy tickets with the money Kate had brought to Malaysia for them.

The others nodded, relieved. The second part of their plan had come through.

Ryan had obtained passports from a contact he had in Singapore and now they could travel without problems.

"When should we call Mark?" Adam asked Ryan.

Ryan was their expert in arranging meetings. Ryan looked around and spotted a few isolated chairs in the corner of the lounge. He waived to them to follow him and they piled onto the chairs around him.

"I think we can do it right now, what are you saying?"

Kate nodded and the guys looked at her, and then at Ryan and approved.

"We'll go with the speaker, okay, so Kate could hear him," Nick said. "Maybe she can tell us what's what. That of course, if we can get through and talk to him, because we couldn't call him from Malaysia at all, you remember."

Ryan approved and dialed Mark's direct number.

After three rings, Mark answered, "Talk to me!"

"Mark, Ryan here."

"Where the hell have you been, you bastard? I've been looking for you everywhere. For months! And where are those two mates of yours, Adam and Nick?" Mark's voice boomed over the phone and Ryan adjusted the volume quickly because a few people had already turned their heads around and looked at them.

"We're all here, and you don't need to shout. We hear you just fine. But if you continue to bellow, the people around will hear you too," Ryan stated calmly.

"Okay, okay, I got it. I'm calm now. You've been off the grid for months. I expected a call, something, but nothing came. What the hell should I have thought? I was told Adam's cover was blown," Mark explained his anguish.

"Yes, it was, but it wasn't much of a cover to begin with. They were waiting for him, man, and he hardly got out with his skin intact. Of course, that didn't last either. When Nick and I came to take him out, they chased us down and Adam was shot."

"Don't tell me that Adam's dead. Ryan, don't tell me that," Mark implored.

The three men looked one to the other in shock. They exchanged inquiring looks because they couldn't believe Mark would get sentimental on them. They'd never heard him talk like that before. Apparently, he did feel something for them.

"He's not dead, but he was close to that. Someone wants us dead, Mark. They had left him alone and hadn't tried to kill him until they had all three of us in their sight," Ryan explained.

"That's what I thought," Mark agreed with his assessment. "Something was strange with that covert op, from the beginning," he told him. "The man who made the plans has disappeared and no one can find him, dead or alive. We're still looking into everything. Anyway, where can we meet?" Mark asked.

"Well, I was thinking it would be a good idea to set up a rendezvous on a neutral ground," Ryan replied. "Like, I don't know… Canada," he proposed as if he'd thought of that just then. "I know we could catch a flight to Montreal or Toronto soon. Wait a minute, let me see."

He muted the phone and said to the others, "We'd better not show our hand and tell him we intended to go to Montreal anyway. Let's let him think we're choosing right now, okay?"

His buddies nodded but Kate intervened, "He's telling the truth, Ryan. He hasn't been involved in this business and he's genuinely stressed with the situation and everything that happened to you three," she said, waving her hand. "When you told him about Adam, that he'd been shot, he hurt. He cares about you all," she reiterated, glancing from one to the other.

"That's great, baby. I'm happy he's not the enemy. But someone might monitor his calls and that's why we couldn't call him from Malaysia. So, if someone's listening into this call right now, we don't want to tip our hand and let them know we're interested in Montreal not Toronto. We'll let them think we chose Montreal for convenience.

Okay? We don't want to lead them to you, Kate. You're not at fault in this," Ryan told her very seriously.

Kate frowned but before she could say anything, Adam intervened, "Not a bad idea, indeed."

He looked at his mates who nodded their approval circumventing Kate's opinion. Their attitude drove her mad but there was no time to tell them what she thought.

Ryan unmuted the cell phone and said, "Mark, Nick says the first connection we have is for Montreal. We'll meet you there in exactly fifty-six hours from now. We'll call you fifteen minutes before the meeting and let you know where we'll be. I don't really know any of the cities up there and I have to check the ground."

"All right, Ryan. Get back safe. All of you, do you hear me?"

"Loud and clear, boss, loud and clear," he replied.

Ryan turned off the phone and, putting into his pocket, told them, "So, time to roll the dice. We'll see how our luck holds. How long until boarding?" he asked Kate.

"Boarding should begin any minute now. We have a long haul to Istanbul and there we have a layover. I think it's two and a half hours or anyway something around that," she explained.

"Good," Adam approved. "Let's find something to eat. I hate plane food," he said bitterly.

"You'll love the lounge in Istanbul," Kate told him. "The food is really something fantastic. I ate so much when I came to Malaysia that I almost couldn't move," she told them and they grinned.

"Great! That's for me," Adam said and led the way to Burger King, craving a big juicy burger with fries. That was something he hadn't had in a while and he couldn't wait to rejoice in the taste.

# CHAPTER NINETEEN

"I think we should rent a car," Nick said, looking around for a rental agency.

"No need," Kate contradicted him. "I have my car parked here in the long-term parking. I think it will fit you all. It's not a girly car, but a big, mean SUV," she continued playfully and the guys started laughing.

"We'd have survived even with a different car, Kate, no worries," Ryan told her and kissed her palm, something he seemed to enjoy doing a lot.

She beamed at him and led them to the parking lot where she'd left her car before taking the plane for Istanbul.

"Ta-da, this is it," she said showing them a sturdy Ford Escape. She was very proud of her car.

"That'll work," Nick said. "Not bad for a girl," he elbowed her and chuckled.

Kate laughed as well and opened the doors and the trunk. They threw their things in the trunk and she started toward the driver side of the car when Ryan stopped her.

"You can call me whatever you want, baby. You can say I'm a damn chauvinist if you want, but I drive. Always."

The woman frowned at him but then, she thought, why not. She was too exhausted to bother herself with driving. She had a GPS in the car, and Ryan could find her place easily. So, without a peep, she handed him the keys and walked around to the other side.

Her attitude dumbfounded Ryan. He'd expected some vocal opposition and prepared an entire tirade. Now he felt cheated.

"You guys, in the back," Kate told Adam and Nick with authority. "I might give him my car keys, but I won't ride in the back," she put her foot down.

The two men grinned and got inside the car without a comment.

Kate input her address into the GPS and turned to the men in the back of the car, "You'll stay all at my place. I have enough space and we'll get food, Adam, don't worry. There are places where we can find food even at this hour. It is quite early," she said checking the time. "We got here at 5:40 and it took us only forty minutes to get out of the airport. It will take us about another twenty or thirty more minutes to get to my house, so it will probably be around seven when we arrive. We can buy food from Metro," she concluded.

"That's a good idea, baby," Ryan agreed with her, "but we're too tired to cook tonight. We need something already cooked, so we could eat, and go immediately to bed and sleep a bit. We need to be in good shape tomorrow morning."

"We can find prepared food at Metro. They have chicken, sausages, various salads, pizza, cakes, whatever you want," Kate answered exuberantly. "Maybe we should stop there before we get home," she proposed. "I'll show you where when we get close, okay?"

Ryan nodded but didn't seem to pay too much attention to what she was saying. He looked preoccupied with something else and kept checking the rear-view mirror.

"Is there something wrong?" Adam asked him.

He knew how Ryan behaved in certain situations, and his attitude was telling him something was going on.

"I think we have some company, guys," Ryan replied in a cool voice and checked the mirror again. He'd been trained to keep a clear mind in dangerous situations. "Actually, I'm pretty sure. How the hell did they find us?" he wondered and a hint of fury and puzzlement colored his voice.

"Probably the call to Mark," Nick replied. "If they have the means for face recognition, it wouldn't have been hard to find us. Remember, Ryan, that was why you sent those photos to Kate. So they couldn't trace your connection to her," Nick reminded him.

Kate's eyes widened, "I always wondered why you sent those photos. I couldn't see anything. It could have been an alien from out of space, for all I knew. I thought you just didn't want me to know how you looked."

"Well, I had to, sweetie. Now, everyone, take care, I will try to lose them, okay? They're already close and I don't want to risk anything," he said and pushed the pedal to the floor, making the car jump forward.

Kate grasped the arm rest and held on for her life. Her breathing became shallow and fear overwhelmed her. She'd never been in such circumstances and the increased speed of the car was enough to make her tremble.

Ryan was a good driver, though. Even in the evening rush, he controlled the car with easiness, while overtaking car after car and moving from lane to lane, setting off a chorus of horns behind him.

He was good, but the car chasing them got closer and closer. Ryan knew he had to find a way to get off the freeway and find narrow streets where he could lose the tail.

He saw an exit coming up. He'd just cut in front of a car, which of course honked them, and aimed for the exit, when he heard the rear window exploding, followed by vicious swearing coming from his mates in the back seats. He swerved onto the exit and despite the speed limit, continued to drive as fast as possible to keep his advantage.

"Is everyone okay?" he asked, when he felt it was safe enough.

He turned his head for a couple seconds. Adam and Nick were brushing shreds of glass off their clothes. Yet, despite a few cuts, they seemed all right and Ryan breathed with relief.

Then Kate's moan reached his ears and his blood ran cold. The explosion had been in the back of the car and the thought of checking on her had never crossed his mind.

"Baby, are you all right? Sweetheart? Come on, talk to me," he said, turning to her and trying to take her hand.

"Watch the road, damn it," Adam bellowed when the car swerved to the right, ready to get onto the shoulder of the road. "I'll see to her."

"The hell you...," Ryan started shouting back but Kate's frightened voice interrupted him.

"Watch the road, Ryan. I think I'm fine. The bullet only grazed my skin, but it hurts, damn it, and I couldn't stop moaning, all right?" she clarified what had happened.

"Are you sure you're fine, Kate?" Ryan asked, his voice shaking.

"I'll be fine if you keep your eyes on the road, Ryan," she screamed when, due to his inattention, the car moved into the oncoming lane.

Luckily, no cars were coming toward them at that moment. Ryan swung the steering wheel and got back on track. He checked the rear-view mirror and saw the other car hadn't made the exit and followed them, which was a blessing.

Still, he couldn't be sure whether they'd taken Kate's plate number or not and that was bad. Apparently, they had the means to find out who she was and come after her.

"Kate, I don't think it's a good idea to go to your house tonight, sweetie," Ryan said in a calm voice not to alarm her beforehand.

"Why not?" she cried. "I want home, Ryan. I want to sleep in my bed tonight," she said stubbornly and her tantrum prompted Adam to roll his eyes.

Nick just watched her as if she'd been a very strange museum exhibit. She had seemed a reasonable woman before that incident.

"Sweetie, if they got the plate off your car, then they know where to find you and, implicitly, all of us," Ryan explained to her patiently, as if he'd been talking to a child.

He considered she was in too much pain and he had to be gentle with her. Ryan was going crazy because he didn't know how bad she was hurt. He wanted to stop the car right there and check her out, but at the same time, he wanted to put as much distance as possible between them and their pursuers. He also tried to decide where they should go so they wouldn't be tracked any further.

Kate looked at him for a few seconds as if she hadn't understood what he was talking about. When comprehension dawned, her face lit up and she said, "No, they can't. I bought this car a week before I left for Malaysia from a guy who went back to his country. I didn't have the time to change the registration or anything. I have only the receipt. No one can track me using the plate of the car and no one can get hurt because that guy took his entire family with him," she explained further. "I understood they'd decided they could do much better back home with what they'd made here than they would have if they'd continued to live in Montreal."

"Are you sure, Kate? Because these guys are ruthless, sweetie, and I don't want you in any kind of danger," Ryan tried to reason with her.

"I'm absolutely positive, Ryan. I even gave those guys a ride to the airport when they left. The car was the last thing they sold."

"I was talking about the registration, Kate," Ryan scowled at her.

"So, you care only about us but not about them," she replied upset.

"I didn't say that. I only asked if you were sure no one can trace the car back to your home," he lost his temper and roared at her.

"Ryan, she's hurt," Nick said calmly. "I don't think yelling at her now is a good tactic."

Kate continued to stare Ryan down belligerently. He merely shook his head and checked the mirror again.

"Okay, we've lost them. So, we're going to your house then," he told her.

She approved nodding and then added, "Of course, we need to buy some food first…"

She didn't manage to finish because Ryan glanced at her in disbelief and asked her, "Are you out of your mind?"

"What now?" she asked with consternation.

There was always something with Ryan and she just couldn't keep up with his moods.

"You're hurt, woman. I need to see how hurt you are and you're thinking of going shopping. Typical female," he finished exasperated.

"What? I'm not talking about going and buying shoes, Ryan. I'm talking about food. It's a strict necessity in any household," she reminded him.

"Out of question," he bit back. "We're going home, look at your wound and decide then."

"Who died and made you the boss?" she asked him heatedly.

Adam coughed discretely and then tapped her on the shoulder softly and said, "He's the boss, Kate. He's always the boss. If he says we're going to your house first, that's what we're doing. Or, if I can suggest something else," he said looking explicitly at Ryan, "either Nick or I, or both, I guess, could go to that Metro thing and buy food and come to Kate's house afterwards. If you tell us where to go, Kate, we can do it. Meantime, you can check her out."

For a few moments, silence reigned in the car. Unable to stand the tension anymore, Kate turned to Ryan and asked sweetly, "Well? Boss? What do you think?"

He narrowed his eyes and looked at her pointedly, and then replied, "All right, Adam. Kate will give you directions to get to that store."

"Wouldn't it be better," Kate inquired always sweetly, something that was already getting under Ryan's skin, "if we drive them to the store, leave them there and I provide the info for them to come to my house? Although," she added turning to Adam "there's some distance to get to my house from the store on foot. It will probably take you about fifteen minutes if not more."

Nick waived his hand to show that the distance was inconsequential for them and she smiled at him despite the pain she was feeling in her left arm. It felt like someone was thrusting a knife into her arm repeatedly and she had to make serious efforts not to moan or cry out in pain. She thought she'd better keep Ryan calm, at least until they got to her house. He seemed easily irascible and she wanted to get home in one piece.

They left the two men at the store and Kate gave them her debit card and PIN number and explained to them how to get to her house from there.

Then, Ryan drove directly to her home, parked the car inside the garage to have it out of sight, and turned to her, "Now, let's go and see how bad you're hurt. It killed me that I had to wait so long before I could see," he confessed and she smiled at him. Her smile was genuine this time.

Kate got out of the car and went straight into the house through a side door, closely followed by Ryan who was carrying all their bags. She showed him to the kitchen where she threw her handbag onto the table and stiffly sat down.

"You can do your worst," she said, stretching her arm toward him.

Ryan saw blood coagulated everywhere and that scared him. He didn't know the exact location of the wound, so he took a kitchen towel and wet it, then came back to clean her arm.

"You want to use my cotton white tea towel to clean the blood on my arm?" she practically roared at him. "Are you out of your mind, Ryan? Do you know I can't take out the blood stains from that? Blood doesn't come out even with bleach," she pointed out.

"Kate, things are just things. This is just a towel. Your arm is more important, I think," Ryan tried to placate her and spoke as calm as possible given the circumstances.

It didn't work. She glowered at him and stood up, "We can clean my arm directly in the sink. We just let the water running over it. There's no need to use my good tea towel," she repeated and went to the sink with determination.

"It's a tea towel, for God's sake. I'll buy you another one, Kate," he said, coming after her.

He couldn't reconcile the woman who generously used so much of her money to help them with the woman who was crying over a blasted towel.

"It won't be the same, Ryan, and you know it. More importantly, I'll know it. Where's the problem if I clean my arm straight under the water jet?" she inquired stubbornly.

"It might hurt a little more," he said, not very certain of that fact, but he had to say something in his defense.

"Huh!" she exclaimed. "It hurts enough now. It can't be worse."

Then she turned on the water, checked the temperature and put her arm under the jet. She yelped suddenly when the water got in contact with her wound.

"I knew you wouldn't listen, Kate. You're too stubborn for your own good, sweetie. Come on, let me clean your arm carefully so we can see what's there," Ryan stroked her cheek and grinned at her, trying to persuade her into doing his bidding.

She looked at him mutinously for a moment, and then she said, "All right, you do it."

Ryan gently took her arm and started washing it, cleaning the blood thoroughly to get to the actual wound. After he wiped all the blood away, he saw the bullet only had grazed her skin. It wasn't very bad but not very good either and his heart cringed. He knew she must have been in serious pain.

"You'll be fine, Kate. Soon, you'll see. We'll need some antibiotic to put on this. I have something in my bag," he said and went to his bag to take out the powdered antibiotic he'd used on Adam. He liberally powdered some over her wound.

He checked her arm carefully again, and pensively said, "I think we'd better cover it with a bandage to be sure it stays clean, all right?"

Kate rolled her eyes, then looked at him and said, "But I need a shower, Ryan, and very, very bad after so many hours spent in planes and airports…"

"Don't worry, baby," Ryan comforted her. "I'll help you shower and I'll take care not to wet the bandage, you'll see. Everything will be just fine."

Kate smiled naughtily at him, knowing what a shower together meant for him but Ryan chuckled at her and said, "Not tonight, baby. You're hurt, I wouldn't do that to you."

"You make it sound like a chore," Kate replied not very satisfied with his answer.

"No, sweetie, it's just that you're hurt and very tired. I'd be a complete asshole to make love to you tonight. I won't make any promises for tomorrow, but tonight, I'll just hold you while you sleep all right? Let's take you out of these clothes and shower you before the guys come back," Ryan said, starting to lift her sleeveless shirt. Then, he allowed her to guide him to the bathroom.

# CHAPTER TWENTY

After an uneventful night and a very satisfying breakfast, at least according to Adam, who apparently liked to eat, Ryan contacted Mark and told him about the adventure they'd had the previous evening.

"I have a very clear idea now who the person of interest might be," Mark told Ryan. "I already have my second-best team looking into this. You know you three are my best team, Ryan... Anyway, they should take care of this business today."

"That's great, Mark," Ryan replied. "By the way, those guys are your best team. We're out of the picture, remember?" he pointed out.

Adam and Nick nodded, and Kate simply beamed at him, happy that he wouldn't be in danger anymore.

"Are you sure, Ryan? Is it because of this fiasco?" Mark inquired, unwilling to let his best men leave.

"You know very well we've already decided not to take any more jobs, Mark.

Before this happened. I want to marry, and Adam..."

"You want to marry," Mark interrupted him in a stunned voice. Then, he started laughing. "How the hell will you marry if you don't even have a woman to marry? You're bullshitting me, man."

"Actually, I do have a woman to marry," Ryan replied and smiled at Kate who was holding his hand. "We'll marry by the end of this weekend, if I have something to say in the matter," he said, continuing to watch Kate and see her reaction.

She grinned at him brightly and nodded her consent. It wasn't as if she hadn't thought of that, especially after he asked her to marry him.

She wanted to marry him because she was sure their lives would never get boring. Why, with their constant bickering and making love and interesting conversations...

No, Ryan was the best choice for her. He had the strength and mind she'd have liked in a man and he could surprise her all the time because she couldn't read his mind.

She'd realized that was what she wanted, even though she didn't know it. She wanted a man like him, someone she couldn't read.

Kate knew she'd have doubts sometimes and maybe occasional if not frequent heartaches, yet it seemed much better than the alternative. She'd have been bored to tears by the end of the month with a man she could read like an open book.

"I seem to have a say in the matter, Mark, so I'll be married by the end of the week, man," Ryan announced with more exuberance than anyone had ever seen him display before.

"And I'm not invited, I surmise," Mark said in a dry voice.

Ryan exchanged looks with Kate and when she agreed, he replied to Mark, "Actually, if you're still in Montreal by the end of the week, yes, we'd like to have you here."

"All right, then. Now you're talking," Mark replied with joy. "Now let me finish with those guys and then we'll meet. Give me a call after a couple hours, Ryan. It should be done by then," Mark said in an implacable voice and disconnected the call.

Ryan looked inquiringly at Kate.

"He's telling the truth, Ryan. He's got a lead and is confident he'll have those people under lock and key in less than two hours."

Nick looked from her to Ryan and back again and said, "We could have used her in the past. Imagine how many bad things we might have avoided having such info."

Adam and Ryan chuckled and then, Ryan leaned and kissed Kate.

"Soon, this will be over, love, and we'll get on with our lives, all right?"

She nodded happily and hugged him, not embarrassed in the least to have spectators to her love.

# EPILOGUE

Kate married Ryan on Saturday morning, August the 3$^{rd}$, in her garden, with a few friends in attendance. She invited only Ellie, Alice and Jeanne, and Ryan had his three friends, Adam, Nick and Mark next to him.

Mark kept his word and caught the men who had pursued them. A few years ago, one of his other teams had gone rogue and when one of their first covert operations had been rendered ineffective by Ryan and his men, they swore revenge.

They'd created the most recent undercover mission with the help of another rogue agent. They had hoped Ryan would accept it and they could take him out.

Her wedding day was as beautiful and as sunny as Kate's disposition. Her friends expected Kate to be nervous and a real nightmare, truth be told, because they knew when Kate was nervous she couldn't control her temper. Surprisingly, she was serene and at peace with everything.

She hadn't been dreaming of that day forever and hadn't made plans. She'd never been so girly. But she felt everything was just right and she was happy she'd found the right man to spend the rest of her life with.

Ryan wasn't the most easy-going man on earth, and she was sure they'd have their share of rows and misunderstandings along the years. Yet, she knew he was exactly what she needed.

In opposition to her sunny disposition, Ryan was a real mess, which was also unexpected.

The man who'd gone into dozens of combat situations with a clear mind and a steady hand, was scared out of his mind now, and his panic showed in his tense eyes.

He was afraid Kate wouldn't like the ring he'd bought for her. He'd chosen something simple because he felt it would suit her, but now he had doubts.

He was also afraid she'd change her mind in the last moment and say *no*. That scared him so much he'd barely breathed until he heard her saying '*I do*'.

Then, his tension disappeared and he became the man everyone knew, confident and calm under pressure.

Adam and Nick looked at him, not recognizing the comrade they'd gone into battle with for over a decade. Nick kept shaking his head and Adam even whispered to Nick, "If I ever get like that, you have free hand to shoot me, man. I won't ever fall in love, I swear. Love seems to make the smartest man as dumb as a doorknob."

Nick laughed and told him, "I'll hold you to that, bro. You'll see."

Adam waved his concerns away and his eyes wandered toward the buffet Kate had prepared for guests. He'd eaten just a few hours earlier but now was hungry and needed a refill.

## Author's Bio

**Rowena Dawn** writes romance, reads thrillers and watches comedies. She likes walking through the woods but insanely loves the sea.

She has a love - hate relationship with her writing and drives her dog crazy whenever she doesn't stop writing to take him out.

# EXCERPT *EYES IN THE DARK*
(BOOK TWO IN THE PERFECT HALVES SERIES)

## PROLOGUE

A thin crowd surrounded the casket and not because of the cold spring rain, which had been pouring for the last twelve hours. Not many people had attended the church service either.

*A funeral in the middle of the week will do that to you*, Diane shook her head with grief. People had jobs and families. She couldn't blame them for their absence.

The pastor's words flew past her ears. She'd never been a religious person and didn't find any comfort in the ritual now, either.

When Diane's eyes had swept over the faces of the few people inside the church moments before, her heart had tightened. Bad luck had taken away her aunt's chance at having the people she'd known for years at her side on this last day.

The late Martha Elgin had been well known and respected in the county. *I never even imagined so many people loved her*, Diane thought and wiped her tears.

The constant string of people, coming to pay their respects during the last three nights of the wake, had impressed Diane MacLean, Martha's only niece.

She only realized the priest had ended the service when people began to move and file before Diane to present their whispered condolences and regrets once again.

Some squeezed her hand with affection while others hugged her, although they'd known her for only a few days. Afterwards, they left the cemetery, huddled under big umbrellas.

They would come to the house later, where Diane, with the help of a catering company, had prepared a last repast in her aunt's honor, scheduled for three in the afternoon.

Soon however, Diane remained alone near the casket, her eyes misty with tears, while two burly young men were waiting impatiently under the canopy of a big oak. They wanted to finish with the burial and find some shelter inside, away from the rain. Their eyes laid squarely on her, willing her to leave already.

Diane whispered her farewell and touched the lid of the black lacquered casket with a shaky hand. She loved her aunt and regretted she hadn't come to visit her for almost three years already. Now, her words fell on deaf ears.

She nodded toward the grave diggers and followed the stone path leading out of the cemetery and to the parking lot. She failed to notice the three men hidden in the shadow of a cluster of trees behind her.

The tallest leaned forward and whispered a few words. Nodding, one of the other two made his way through the trees to the same parking lot.

The man beat Diane to the punch. Comfortably seated in his car, he watched her coming up the trail slowly.

She seemed tired and didn't care about the rain, even though her umbrella didn't shield her very well from it. The remote look in her eyes betrayed her scattered thoughts.

Diane didn't notice the man in the car. She placed the umbrella in the trunk of her SUV and hurried to the driver's side.

She drove away, oblivious to the other car, which was trailing her closely now. She drove under the speed limit, although she was expected in town. Her aunt's lawyer had invited her to the reading of the will.

*I already told him I might be late. What's the rush after all? The will won't change.*

# CHAPTER 1

The air tumbled in his lungs and he tasted the smell of the earlier rain in the air. The smell of wet leaves, rustled by the wind all over the forest floor, invigorated him.

He watched the woman closely from underneath the shade of the trees where he'd found a good spot to hide.

*It's just a necessity*, he lied to himself. He knew he liked what he saw. His imagination already roamed on paths he knew he should have avoided.

He held still, afraid he would make a noise by stepping on the twigs that littered the floor of the forest and give his position away. He had enough time to make his presence known and didn't want to scare her before the time was right. He'd outlined a plan and never strayed from a well-thought-out plan.

His eyes roved over the woman's body. Her neck arched and reminded him of a deer at a watering hole at dawn, sniffing the air to feel the hunter lurking.

He grinned. *Yep, sweetheart, you sense me here, but you're not sure. Yet.*

Fatigue had etched visible lines at the corner of her eyes and around her mouth. He'd been watching her for a few hours now and had seen her working hard as she tried to put the ranch house to rights.

The wind teased him with a faint whiff of green apples and lemon, stirring long-forgotten memories. He bristled and scowled the memories away.

The woman shivered and rubbed her arms. The night air was getting cooler.

Her rich coppery hair hung in a messy ponytail. Wisps of hair framed her face and made her look vulnerable.

Suddenly, the man decided he'd watched his fill. '*Show time,*' he said under his breath and stepped out from his hiding place.

"Hey, you over there!"

She almost jumped a feet up when the rough voice whipped through the air. It came from the left side of the yard where lots of bushes and tall trees darkened the night even more. Her wide eyes turned there and caught the glimpse of a tall shadow moving in the dark and a flash of fear seized her breath.

The man closed the distance between them, a grin in the corner of his mouth. Something close to satisfaction bubbled in his veins.

Her eyes widened even more when his tall and broad shape seemed to engulf the space. The fear in her eyes stirred an unknown emotion deep inside him. He tried to label it, but came out empty.

He ruled out compassion although he couldn't explain why. It wasn't as if he had even remembered how compassion felt like.

For a few tense moments, they stared at each other intensely. Neither one moved.

Fear flickered in her green eyes again. A huge male was striding through her yard as if he'd owned the damn place.

His steely black eyes reflected his innate boldness, laced with a hint of amusement and a feral sliver of unidentified hunger. That hunger troubled her. She didn't care about his amusement or anything else.

They assessed each other like two swordsmen.

*Why the heck didn't I listen to my instincts?* She'd thought herself alone out there at the small ranch house, yet, all evening, she had the feeling that someone was watching her. The sensation had electrified the fine hair at the nape of her neck but she'd foolishly dismissed it.

The ranch was far from any crowded roads, which was fine with her. She didn't need legions of people around and she didn't miss the noises of a big city.

Since the death of her aunt, a few months before, she'd been thinking of moving out of town and making a life for herself there, in the middle of nowhere. A week ago, she'd finally done it. Now, she doubted she'd made the right decision.

"I've got a gun, right here," she shouted at him. Her voice shook. "And I know how to use it," she continued in a shrilling voice. Fear almost smothered her and she hardly pushed the words out of her mouth.

His brash laughter reached her ears and her blood ran cold. *He doesn't believe me*, she thought with a shock and for a fleeting moment, she regretted she hadn't taken those self-defence classes she'd been thinking about back then when she was living in the city. *Well, too bad. It's too late to cry over spilled milk now. Time to face the music.*

"Yeah, I bet you do," he hollered back, laughing louder. "Sweetheart," he drawled, and honey dripped off his lips, betraying a specific southern accent, "I'm sure you could darn shoot me if you wanted to. But I doubt you do," he continued and lifted an eyebrow, as if he'd dared her. "I just want help for one night, maybe two, tops," he lied boldly through his teeth.

His fake sweet voice made her fear step aside. Anger took its place and climbed up to her lips at his biting sarcasm.

"Town's in that direction," she replied, pointing to his left. "There, you can find all the help you want, mister," she added in clipped words. "There's nothing here for you," she clarified with a sharp gesture.

"I don't feel like going into town right now," he shrugged. "I'm tired. I've been walking long enough. My car broke down a few miles back down that road, and I need a place to stay. I think I like this one," he said in a flat voice, which brought shivers up her spine.

Then, he came closer and under the spot of light from the veranda.

"How dare you?" she pushed through her tight lips with difficulty. Her hands fisted and her nails bit into her palms.

He was rather tall, a bit too tall for her taste. If he'd been shorter, she might have had a chance to fight him back. He was also much heavier than she was. His build reminded her of a fighter. *This guy's bad news, Diane,* she thought.

"Be a good Christian girl," he said sweetly. "You won't let a poor man outside in the night, here, in the forest, to fend for himself alone, cold and hungry, will you now?" he asked her with a charming smile and opened his arms wide, taunting her.

"I certainly would," she replied and braced her hands on her hips.

She wanted him to understand his words wouldn't move her. She wasn't a simpleton. The times when people opened their doors to strangers were long gone. Anyway, she was a city girl. That habit wasn't in her make-up.

He stepped closer and reached the stairs of the veranda, undeterred by her refusal. He braced one arm on the handrail. His smiling eyes assessed her resolve.

His eyes pleaded innocence, yet she could read toughness behind his smile. She knew he was far from what he wanted her to believe.

The man was built like the rangers she'd read about. Over six feet tall, his eyes were on the same level with hers, even though he was at the foot of the stairs. His shoulders were broad enough to carry her away if he felt like it.

*Oh boy, oh boy*, she mumbled in her mind. She had to do something and get rid of him.

*Damn my urge to admire the night. If I'd been inside, at least I'd have had a door between this bear of a man and me... Although I don't think a locked door would make too much of a difference if he wanted in*, she thought, her eyes taking in the rough maleness before them.

"Come on, missy, don't be a bitch," he tried to cajole her. "I need only one bed for the night," he tried to persuade her, always with that smile, which got on her nerves. "I promise it won't be yours," he added.

She noticed his smile never reached his eyes. The man's eyes were two black arrows trained on her, surveying her every movement. Chips of ice sparkled inside his dark pupils, chilling her to the bone.

His evident sarcasm crawled on her skin and his nonchalant attitude scared her more because she didn't understand his game.

"Are you crazy or what?" she replied with anger in her voice.

"Or what, I think," he softly answered back.

"How could you think I'd let you sleep in my house?" she said furiously.

*It's like she wants to spit on me and be done with me*, he mused. *Not so easily done, honey. The game's over when I say it's over. Now, be a good girl and give in. I won't bother you... too much.*

"All right, then your barn, what about that?" he offered a compromise.

*It's not like I can't afford it for the moment. You'll play a different tune tomorrow, honey.*

"You can lock your doors tonight, and tomorrow, we'll talk some more.

What do you say? It seems like a good trade to me," he shrugged again and tapped the cowboy hat, he had in his hand, on his thigh.

She didn't like his words and was afraid to think about what sort of trade he was talking about. *Yeah, like a locked door would stop you from coming in.*

However, she knew she was at a disadvantage. If she wanted to end that ludicrous discussion, she had to accept his offer and hope he would keep to the barn.

"Go to the barn and wait for me," she said brusquely. "I'll bring you some blankets so you won't feel the cold of the night. All right?"

He smiled at her again, but this time, he showed her two rows of perfect, big, white teeth. His smile reminded her of a wolf in front of its prey, and she shivered.

Then, he bowed mockingly and turned around to go to the barn erected on one side of the big yard.

She didn't move until a metallic squeak reached her ears, letting her know he'd opened the rusty barn door.

Then, she ran inside and belatedly locked the door behind her. It was pointless, but she needed that blanket of security for a moment.

She hadn't forgotten she had to go back out there with the blankets she'd promised. She had to give him some food as well. She couldn't do otherwise if she wanted to avoid his coming to the house to ask, but she couldn't make her feet move. Her legs shook so badly that she needed to lean on the wall to keep herself standing.

Finally, the fear that he might come back forced her to move and she climbed the stairs to the second floor. With shaking hands, she took two blankets from the linen cupboard in the hallway upstairs.

Then, she raided the kitchen and prepared three large sandwiches. *Better safe than sorry*, she thought.

It took her longer than she expected, but then, she kept dropping things. Her fingers shook and she couldn't control them. She took a can of soda out of the fridge and headed to the front door.

Her heart beat faster. She was so scared that she practically jumped out of her skin. Before opening the door, she cautiously moved the flimsy drapes, which covered the side window, and looked out, carefully.

The light in the barn was on, but she couldn't see anything else. *I hope he's waiting for me there and not here.*

Her only other choice was to call the sheriff, but by the time he'd have made it there, she could have been fodder for the vultures.

She opened the door and went out into the dark. In a few long strides, she reached the door of the barn and shouted, "Mister, are you there?"

# EXCERPT BECKA'S AWAKENING

*(BOOK ONE IN THE WINSTONS SERIES)*

## PROLOGUE

"Come on, man, this is so not right!" Josh exploded.

He threw his fork back onto the plate and made his aunt, Marjorie, frown. She loved that set of dishes and feared that the young man's frustrations would sooner or later put a crack in them.

"You're complaining, huh?" Maggie waved her fork at him in mockery and rolled her eyes. "You're still fairly young compared to some of us and you have enough time ahead of you, so you shouldn't be the one complaining!" she retorted angrily.

"He has the right to complain, Maggie, as well as any one of us!" Becka replied in support of her cousin. "So what if we are younger? We're all in the same boat!" she punched the table with her little fist. "Auntie, can't we do something about this?"

"I know you want to, pumpkin, but there's nothing you can do about it," Aunt Marjorie stroked her arm in an attempt to soothe her. "What must be done, must be done!"

"So, we have to pay for something that happened a hundred years before we were even born? How does that make any sense at all?" Alex snapped and joined the others in voicing his outrage, though it didn't stop him from scarfing down another piece of pie.

"It's less than a hundred, you nitwit!" Lily replied with disdain and punched his arm.

"Who the hell cares?" Alex retorted with his mouth full.

He never did learn not to talk with his mouth full, try as his parents might. Anyway, he wouldn't have given a rat's ass on such things, anyway, especially at home.

"One hundred, two hundred, same shit, pardon my French. You know what? I don't feel like paying for some jackass's mistakes!" he ended his heated speech, his finger still pointed at Lily.

"So, what do you propose to do, then?" Matt, who had kept his mouth shut until then, asked with nonchalance.

He had been sipping from his glass of whiskey quietly, with a detached expression on his face that suggested that nothing they discussed could affect him.

"Don't tell me you're okay with this!" Alex answered back in disbelief. "Come on, Matt! You're the oldest, man, and you've only got one year left. You've got to be as angry as I am, if not more! Don't pretend it doesn't bother you because that's not possible!"

Matt took a few moments of silence, sipped a little more from his glass, then looked at Alex and shook his head.

"Angry? Maybe. Can I do something about it? I don't think so," he replied to his cousin with his usual coolness, his eyes gazing steadily at him. "So why should I bother?"

No one had anything to say to that. They were all aware there was one stipulation they had to fulfill and only then they could get their trust funds and also reach their full potential.

The worst part was they had to do so before turning thirty-five, because once one of them turned thirty-five without fulfilling that condition, their share of the fund would be divided among the remaining younger ones who still had time to succeed or fail.

"You know what? I don't really care about unlocking my powers," Ariel said pensively, without addressing anyone in particular, "although, it would be nice to see what you can do if you use your full potential..." she continued, lost in her thoughts as always.

Her cousins gave her time to get to the point. They knew she had the bad habit of rambling on and on or getting lost in her own thoughts only to leave everyone hanging. Yet, sometimes, if not most of the time, she could come up with some very interesting solutions if they had the patience to listen to her.

"But I do care about doing something for myself. I'd like to open a little business..." Ariel finally said longingly.

"Keep dreaming, girl," Maggie snapped, already bored with the way Ariel always liked to drag things out. She wasn't one for patience and, unfortunately, that trait had had some unpleasant results in her daily life. "Till you take care of your part of business, Ariel, girl, you won't be able to open a shed."

"Why are you always so mean to her?" Alex snapped at Maggie. "If she wants to dream, let her dream away. What else can she do? What else is there for any of us?" he asked, his infuriated gaze scanning each one of them to see their reactions.

"Beat the curse?" Marjorie asked softly, trying to defuse a potentially explosive situation.

"Not so easy, auntie," Ariel said sorrowfully. "I tried, you know... Do you remember? I thought that guy, Eric, the one I met two years ago, would be the one. It wasn't meant to be, you know... It's not so easy, and you know it very well. You see how things are. There's no real romance left in this world, I'm afraid. If there's no romance left, where can one find true love?"

Marjorie nodded. She did know it. Finding true love wasn't easy-peasy. She'd been in the same situation when it was her turn and she'd almost lost everything because of her own stubbornness and her family's meddling.

"It's never easy, my dear, I know," she answered and stroked the young woman's arm with love again. "But, Ariel, sweetheart, you have to keep trying. You can't simply give up. Think about it! You will be able to use your powers and get your money, but only once you find your true love and commit to it. You'll be truly happy then!"

Ariel turned her eyes to her plate on the table. She knew her eyes would show everyone she'd already resigned herself and she was sick of hearing platitudes and encouragements whenever her family got wind of something like that.

Everybody around the table remained silent for a few moments. Jay helped himself to some more of his mother's amazing pie.

Marjorie was the best cook in their family, which was why they always chose to meet at her house. Everything was easier to swallow if there was a good pie or cake on the table. At least, in Jay's opinion.

"I think we should see if there's any legal way to get out of this situation, guys. We need the money now, don't we? It's not like we can wait around forever!"

Alex broke the silence, when the idea came to him suddenly. His eyes analyzed them carefully and saw them nod their assent. "Look," he continued, "I'm already thirty-two. I don't have time for stupid things and games and all sorts of idiotic attempts at love! I want to do something for myself like Ariel said. Now, while I still can."

Although almost everybody found themselves in agreement with him, they still looked at Matt. He was known to be the smartest guy in the family and they knew that any kind of solution should have come from him. Matt's eyes shifted around the table, feeling their expecting gazes on him and finally shook his head.

"There's no way out, buddy," Matt put his glass on the wooden table at the same time and stood from the bench. "If you called us here just for this discussion, then I'm out of here. I've got real things to do, places to see…"

"You don't even want to try," Becka cried out, jumping out of her seat. "You've just given up because you have so little time left and you don't care anymore."

"I tried, sweetie," Matt told her with a sad smile on his lips.

Becka was his favorite cousin. Maybe because she was the youngest or maybe because she was unspoiled and funny and had a very big heart. His fingers stroked her cheek in a loving, yet sad caress, and he kissed her forehead.

"Becka, I tried hard to find any kind of loophole in the wording of the trust funds papers. Believe me, there's none. If I couldn't find one, sweetie, then no one can, and you know it. There's a reason I'm one of the best attorneys in the country, and all of you know this isn't just my vanity talking. Anyway, honey, these days, I content myself with making my own money the hard way and enjoying as much as possible the little spare time I have left. I've stopped chasing such dreams. It's not in the cards for me and that's it."

All of his cousins looked at him in shock. Only his sister, Maggie, understood him very well. She didn't have any patience, especially with fools, but Matt was something special.

She'd always looked up to him and she knew he wasn't the kind of guy to give up on anything without a fight. Hearing him say he'd resigned himself made her understand the depth of his anger, even though he hid it from them.

She felt like taking him into her arms and never letting go but she knew he wouldn't like that. He wasn't very big on displays of affection, her brother, so she just lightly petted his hand and left it at that.

"Matt, you should try to use that time you have left to find a girl," his mother said reproachfully and everyone's attention turned to Marjorie, who continued, "You still have a chance, son, and I'm not talking about the money here, you know it. I know that sad affair with Velma's left you afraid to commit again and I don't like that in the least. That's not the Matty I know. That wasn't love, son, and you know it. Had it been true love, you'd have had your full powers by now even if you hadn't gotten the money."

"Mother, Velma's been out of the picture for a decade already. She's in the past. What's the point in bringing her back into the conversation?" Matt retorted curtly, shaking his head. He couldn't understand his mother's reasons for bringing up bitter memories.

"Because she was the reason you stopped looking at women with hope," Marjorie pointed out, shaking a scolding finger at her first born. "You think all women are like her and that's why you just take everything you can from them and move on. Another woman on the list! It's like you're keeping a score: how many women can Matt score?" she reproached acidly, which wasn't something that they'd witnessed before. Everyone's eyes were riveted on her. "It's not good for you, Matt! Even if you've already given up on the trust fund, which is stupid, by the way, you're still alive and you still need a reliable woman in your life, like I've already said over and over again. You'll grow old and alone and bitter!" Marjorie ended her unusual tirade by punching her son's chest with her finger.

"Thanks for the heads up, mom. It's always good to know what your future will look like!" Matt replied sarcastically and removed himself from the path of her pointy finger. Yet, he didn't leave. He seemed undecided and glance back at his cousins.

Marjorie shook her head bitterly, but chose not to continue that line of discussion. She knew her son quite well and she knew there was no way to make him change his mind when he was like that. It was like talking to a rock.

The silence stretched for a few minutes. Everyone was busy either eating their pie or playing with their drinks, pretending nothing out of ordinary had happened between Marjorie and her eldest son. But mostly, they were busy avoiding each other's eyes for fear someone might say something hurtful again.

In the end, Alex, the most outspoken of all, couldn't stand the awkward silence anymore and looked around the table, gauging everyone's mood. Uncertain whether it was even worth it, he shrugged and decided to try a new line of conversation.

"You know, you are the old lady's favorite great-grandson, Matt. Can't you persuade her to end this foolishness? She can change the papers if she wants to. It's not like the words are carved in stone!" Alex anxiously waited for his answer.

"Tried that too, Alex." Matt sighed, shaking his head. "She said she did it for our own good, whatever she means by that. So… I can say I've tried everything and it's time to limit my losses."

Again, no one said anything for a few moments and, again, they couldn't bring themselves to look each other in the eye and the silence stretched on.

Encouraged by the unusual silence, since such get-togethers were normally a very chatty and loud affair, Matt took his leave with a simple wave of his hand and started down the path to the kitchen door, whistling softly to himself.

Ariel, pensive as always, looked after him until he was out of earshot, and said dolefully, "It's sad… It's really sad. He's the oldest and he's already given up."

For a few moments, everyone stared at her absolutely speechless. It was like she'd grown a second head during the last hour.

"Well, we're close to that too, Ariel," her brother Alex retorted angrily after a moment of disbelief. "It's not like we have too much time left, is it? Just about three years, you dimwit! Once we turn thirty-five, everything will be gone: the money, the powers, everything. And we can't do a single thing to stop this!"

"We can't even cheat," Jay intervened bitterly for the first time and the others burst into laughter.

"Oh, yeah, I remember," Lily said. "You tried to pose as a fool in love and came with that simpleton. Camilla, I think her name was?"

Jay nodded smiling. He had already forgotten the ridicule he'd suffered at the time. His easy-going nature didn't allow him to keep a grudge for long.

"Yeah, but it didn't work, did it?" Josh said very matter-of-factly. "Those two fossils sniffed you out."

"Well, they can read minds, so it was a piece of cake to sniff him out," Aunt Marjorie pointed out with an enigmatic smile on her lips. "That's why they've been appointed trustees, you know. No one can fool them. You shouldn't have tried to cheat, Jay. The old lady hasn't forgiven you for that yet."

Jay shrugged. He knew very well where he stood with his grandma those days. He didn't think she would ever forgive him.

The old bat was a real piece of work. She was resentful and bitter.

Just a few of them could steal a smile from her and lately he hadn't been part of that group. After the stunt he had pulled with that woman, grandma didn't even acknowledge him at the family dinners anymore. She pretended he didn't even exist.

He looked around and noticed all the others had gone quiet, each of them thinking about the implications of what had happened to him.

He truly hoped he wouldn't go through a new period of veiled mean jokes or even innocent teasing. At which Becka was a master. He even flinched when she started speaking, expecting the worst.

"So, we only have to wait for them to die..." Becka tentatively began to say, her gaze passing from one to the other.

"Not so fast," Marjorie interrupted her hastily. "The rule says that if they pass away, two others will take their place. Same type of power, pumpkin, so no way to fool them either. You have to understand there is no way around this. You have to play by the rules."

"Damn it!" Alex swore. "All this drama only because great-grandpa had the nerve to abandon great-grandma for another woman and then another idiot left aunt Evelyn at the altar and she killed herself!" he shook his head as if everything was inconceivable for him. "So, now, generation after generation has to pay for those two idiots! Where the hell is the justice in that?"

"Well, I think it was a radical conclusion from my grandmother, as well," Marjorie replied conciliatorily, "but there's never been a way to change grandma's mind, unfortunately. I know my father tried hard at the time, but she wouldn't listen to him. He tried again when my happiness was at stake and still nothing. He didn't have any success. She wouldn't give in. Not even a bit. Since the money was still hers, she had the right to decide what she wanted to do with it."

"But why the curse on our powers? I really don't understand that," Becka wondered.

"Same reason. Grandpa was a witch himself and he used those powers to entice a very young woman and leave grandma. And the man who left Evelyn at the altar was also enticed by a witch. She didn't want any other witch to misuse their powers."

"I wouldn't!" Becka cried out.

"I know you wouldn't, pumpkin," Marjorie patted her hand tenderly. "Not all apples are rotten, I know that much. But grandma didn't want to hear a thing, so… Here we are: now, everyone in my generation paid for that and yours has to pay, as well. However, if you succeed in finding your true love and get your trust funds, then at least the money problem will end and the next generations will have only the curse to defeat," Marjorie tried to lift their moods, but with little success.

"Oh, just that," Lily sighed and put her chin in her hand, fixing her dreamy gaze somewhere in the distance.

"I really wanted to open that nursery," Ariel whispered inconsolably and her brother stroked her fingers, his eyes shining with deep concern for his sister's dreams.

"Nothing is lost, sweetheart," Marjorie said and stroked Ariel's hand at her turn. "You'll see. You'll find your soul mate, Ariel. Everything will be fine."

"Where? Where could I find my soul mate, auntie? The people I deal with every day are not even lover material, believe me. I wouldn't let them touch me with a ten-foot pole, so finding a soul mate is quite out of question. There's no chance for me out there! I've looked around for years and nothing!" she said, this time with tears in her eyes.

"Wait and see, Ariel. These things have a way of working out," Marjorie whispered to her, then started picking up their plates to show them that the conversation ended.

There was no point in debating something they couldn't fix. There wasn't anything more to add and whining wouldn't help. The older woman knew it well. Whining never helped. You had to roll up your sleeves and do something.

Although the others jumped out of their seats to help her, they were all still thinking about the conversation and a none-too-rosy future, which looked pretty hopeless for them at that very moment.

# CHAPTER ONE

Becka left the coffee shop in a hurry. She was holding a hot coffee cup in one hand, while, at the same time, she was trying to stick a muffin and a toasted bagel in her handbag with the other.

She'd forgotten to ask for a hot sleeve for the cup and on top of that, she'd also forgotten to take a napkin. Her head was deep in the clouds that morning, and now, the searing heat burned her fingers through the paper cup.

She couldn't go back to the coffee shop. She was already late for her morning classes and the last thing she wanted was to miss the entire lecture on her favorite subject.

Becka kept struggling. She tried to make the muffin and bagel fit in her handbag, at which point she wondered why she'd left the house with such a tiny purse.

The people and things around her became a blur the more she wrestled with the bag and the more she rushed toward the bus stop.

No more than a moment later, just as she turned around the corner, her eyes still on the tiny handbag that wouldn't cooperate with her, she ran into a tall man and as luck would have it, the lid of the coffee cup came loose and all the hot liquid spilled all over the giant's pristine, white shirt.

Of course, Becka thought, things couldn't get any worse! Not only did she scald him but the damn shirt had to be white! Why not black? No one would notice a coffee stain on a black shirt!

"Oh, my God, I'm so sorry! Really, really, sorry!" she blabbered and tried to clean his shirt with her bare hands, forgetting about the cup lying on the pavement, discarded like yesterday's news, all but empty. She'd also forgotten about her coveted breakfast, which was leaning precariously on one side of the handbag, ready to fall out as well.

Her hands shook the man's shirt as fast as she possibly could. Her meager attempts hoped to limit the burns at the very least.

Becka knew the hot coffee must have already penetrated his shirt and she didn't even want to think of what had happened to the skin beneath it, badly burnt by the freshly boiled brew.

"I think you'd better take your shirt off!" she cried out, without taking her gaze off the task at hand.

Remorse drove her actions. Images of the emergency room flashed at the back of her mind. Focused to a frenzy on her nearly catastrophic mistake, Becka never noticed the rest of the man to whom the chest belonged, much less the eyebrow which shot up as soon as she ordered him to strip.

"May I ask what exactly you're trying to do?" he finally asked in a deceptively mild tone.

Until then, he'd simply looked at the top of her head, completely shocked by the actions of the little woman before him.

Hearing his voice, she finally looked up and blinked. Not once or twice, but three times. The man she had in front of her wasn't the regular polished and polite man she'd encountered in her life before. He was a far, far cry from that.

This man's rugged face was set off by a long, pale scar on his left cheek that began somewhere close to the corner of his eye and continued to nearly the corner of his mouth, giving him a dangerous allure. He looked like one of the mercenaries she had seen in one of the documentaries about the civil war in former Yugoslavia. It wasn't reassuring.

His eyebrow was still raised scornfully and for a moment there, she asked herself how he did it. It wasn't easy to pull off that move for so long, she imagined. The young woman just about forgot her curiosity when she met his eyes, colder than the Arctic Ocean. She almost shivered.

She blinked again, swallowed hard and tried to find her voice. She forced herself to be brave, refusing to even consider the thought of being a scaredy-cat. She'd always tried to face any danger, not run away from it, and that wasn't the moment to change her ways.

"Hmm.... I was thinking... you know... your shirt..."

"I heard that bit about my shirt, don't you worry, but I really don't know what difference you think it would make if I took it off now. With or without the shirt, my skin is still scalded, my morning's still ruined and I'm still pissed off…" he said in a level tone, which didn't show the slightest hint of anger and that made her even more fearful.

While it was true he didn't sound mad, the complete clash between his words and his tone made her nervous. Becka couldn't even begin to think of how to talk to him.

She swallowed again and bravely said, "Yes, I know that, but the coffee is mostly on the shirt, so if you take it off…"

"Now?" he mused, when he saw she stopped without finishing her sentence.

"Well, yes," she nodded and stressed her words, in an effort to lend them more confidence than she had.

She pretended she knew what she was doing, although her face was burning in absolute embarrassment and shame.

It was the first time she'd ever asked a man to take his clothes off, even though it was only the shirt. On top of all that, his tone and attitude made her terribly uncomfortable and she was afraid that everything showed on her face.

She couldn't say she had a poker face worth a damn. Every time she played cards with Jay, he would laugh at her best, yet failed efforts to bluff.

The man looked at her for a few seconds, but then, with a bold move, he took his shirt off.

"Do your worst!" he said and handed her the all but ruined piece of clothing.

However, Becka didn't take it. She didn't even notice he was holding anything for her to take. She couldn't even find her voice to answer back. Her eyes were too busy taking in the expanse of a chiseled chest peppered with curly coarse hair, still wet from her coffee. She'd forgotten what she wanted or was supposed to do entirely.

"Earth to the moon?" he mocked her in his grave voice and waved his hand before her eyes.

Finally, his gestures pulled her out of her reverie and Becka's eyes shot up to meet his in an instant.

"Sorry, just lost in thought for a moment there," she mumbled more than a little disappointed with her silly admiration of the male figure. She'd thought herself above such trivial endeavours.

Finally, she took the shirt from his waiting hand and used it to dry his chest more vigorously than it was necessary.

The coffee was already a dry sticky stain, but that wasn't on her mind and neither was the fact that she might take off a layer of vulnerable, burned skin, too.

None of those things dawned on her because, to be truthful, Becka was brimming with embarrassment, upset with herself for her carelessness and every reaction that followed.

Not only had she poured her coffee all over a stranger but she'd been caught staring at the man's chest like a lustful, simple-minded woman.

"Yeah, I noticed," he replied amused, watching her expression while she cleaned his chest.

The man enjoyed her train of thought. He could read it on her face with no effort whatsoever.

It was refreshing to see someone so unspoiled like the woman before his eyes. He was tired of all the games played in society and wanted something new.

After a few moments, he decided to ask, "Does any man's chest have this effect on you or just mine?"

There was a little malice in his voice and that made her straighten up and look directly into his eyes. Then, she replied sulkily, "I'm just trying to help, you know! Why are you acting like a jerk?"

When she snapped at him, his eyes became colder than they had been before and he yanked the shirt out of her hands.

"Yeah, with such help I wouldn't be surprised if I'm dead tomorrow!"

She tapped her foot in frustration, raised her voice a notch, and replied to him with her usual self-confidence, "You're just pissed off because I ruined your shirt."

Her voice mustered all the determination she could and she added a nod, for good measure, in the hopes it would give her more of a knowledgeable air.

"But it was just an accident, you have to understand. It wasn't like I wanted to spill my coffee all over you! I'd have preferred to drink it, you know," she scoffed and shrugged her shoulders.

She was standing tall before him, matching his confident, dominant attitude with her own, but spoiled everything when she continued in the tone of a stubborn and willful child, "I really could have used that coffee!"

Fascinated with the sudden change in her attitude, he looked at her more attentively. Only now, he noticed her chocolate eyes and especially her little mouth, arched like a bow, with rosy lips. A part of him was almost begging and pushed him to grab her already and just have a taste of her sweet, sensual mouth.

The longer she talked, his interest in her lips only grew more and he got to the point of an agonizing need urging him to lean in and claim what he wanted. He found them more tempting when the tip of her tongue came out and nervously licked her upper lip. Something stirred inside him and, suddenly, his interest changed completely.

"You owe me," he said so abruptly that it charged the atmosphere in an instant.

Becka opened her mouth in shock to reply. Yet, she couldn't make a sound for a few moments. She was too stunned by his sudden outburst.

The man didn't clarify his statement or expand on it. He just waited for her to process his words and get back to him with a bold retort. From what he'd seen so far, he was sure to get one. He didn't have to wait for too long.

"What are you talking about?" she finally managed to say, with a touch of thinly veiled indignation, and her wide eyes held his own intently.

"What you heard," he brushed off her harmless furor and continued, "You owe me."

"For this shirt?" she asked incredulously, showing him the shirt she held in her hand.

"Among other things."

His wolfish smile ran shivers down her spine, as her mind started dreading the worst and conjured unsettling scenarios.

"What other things?" Becka asked, although more than a little hesitation and uncertainty delayed her question.

Her eyes seemed to grow wider still and the tip of her tongue again touched her upper lip nervously, to torment him and make him more aware of his increasing desire for her.

He couldn't understand that irrational, unlikely desire for a clumsy woman he'd just laid eyes on, but something in him wanted her. He actually needed to have her, just like that.

She looked a bit young, maybe too young, that was true enough, but he knew that looks were sometimes deceptive. He still made a mental note to ask her about her age. He didn't want to fool around with jailbait even though he was agonizingly drawn to her.

He had a strict policy about going to jail. His policy was simple enough. Jail wasn't a place he ever yearned to see on the inside. He did once and even once in a lifetime was more than enough.

"You scalded me, ruined my shirt, and obviously, I can't go to my appointment half-naked. And, please, note, it's an important appointment, and I'm already late because of you," he explained patiently, as if he'd been talking to a small child.

Of course, it was all just a ruse. He was only trying to see what kind of reaction he could draw from her.

She felt the blood rush to her face and she cursed her pale complexion that revealed too much and in the most inappropriate of moments.

No matter how much she tried to appear sophisticated or cool-tempered, she always failed because her skin betrayed her. It was the curse of her life. Maybe not the only curse she had to contend with but it made the top three.

Becka thought of going a different way with him, to get herself out of the trouble that seemed to be brewing, and, very politely, said, "I'm very sorry for scalding you and for ruining your shirt. Of course, I'm sorry about your appointment as well, but I don't see how I could…"

She never finished her sentence because she saw a naughty smile flourish on his lips. That made her lose her train of thought again. This time she was afraid of what he'd say.

"I think you owe me something and you can set it right by going on a date with me," he finally specified his conditions in a tone implying too many things that would better remain unsaid.

"A date with you." she repeated automatically as if she weren't able to grasp the concept.

This series *Perfect Halves* will have four books and all of them will be about love, adventure and conspiracies. You have met all male characters in this first novel.

Look for Book Two in Rowena Dawn's "*Perfect Halves*" series: **EYES IN THE DARK.** Book Three **PULLED IN** Coming soon!

*Also by Rowena Dawn:*

Leap of Faith

Becka's Awakening (Book One in The Winstons Series)

Mr. (Almost) Right

Matt's Dilemma (Book Two in The Winstons Series)

*Forthcoming:*

Jay's Salvation (Book Three in The Winstons Series)

Thank you for taking the time to read *Double-Edged*, the first book in the series *The Perfect Halves*.

If you enjoyed it, please consider telling your friends or posting a short review.

Word of mouth is an author's best friend and much appreciated. Thank you,
*Rowena Dawn*

www.ingramcontent.com/pod-product-compliance
Lightning Source LLC
Chambersburg PA
CBHW070129080526
44586CB00015B/1621